Getting a job in
Canada

If you want to know how...

Living & Working in Canada
A practical guide to life in Canada

Getting a Job Abroad
The international jobseekers' directory

Getting into Canada
How to make a successful application for permanent residence

Getting a Job in America
A step-by-step guide to finding work in the USA

howtobooks

Send for a free copy of the latest catalogue to:

How To Books
3 Newtec Place, Magdalen Road,
Oxford OX4 1RE, United Kingdom
email: info@howtobooks.co.uk
http://www.howtobooks.co.uk

Getting a job in
Canada

REVISED AND UPDATED
5TH
FIFTH EDITION

Valerie Gerrard

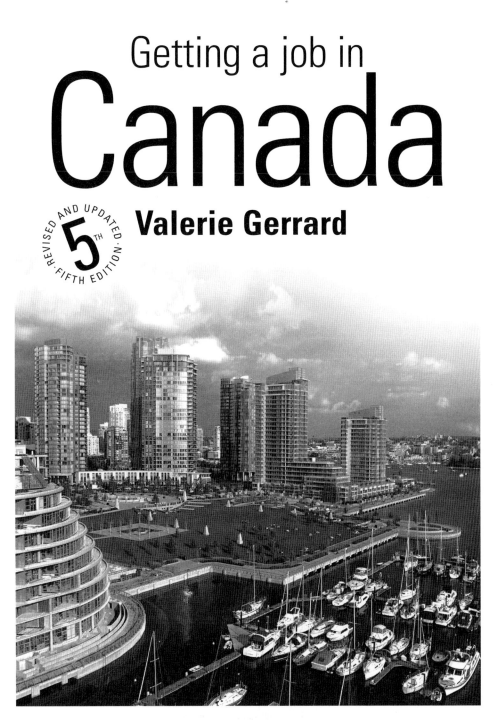

REVISED: FULLY UPDATED & EXTENDED TEXT

howtobooks

First published by How To Books Ltd, 3 Newtec Place,
Magdalen Road, Oxford OX4 1RE. United Kingdom.
Tel: (01865) 793806. Fax: (01865) 248780.

Second edition 1999
Third edition 2002
Fourth edition 2004
Fifth edition 2006

British Library Cataloguing in Publication Data
A catalogue record for this book is available from the British Library

Cover design by Baseline Arts Ltd, Oxford
Produced for How To Books by Deer Park Productions, Tavistock
Typeset by PDQ Typesetting, Stoke-on-Trent, Staffs.
Printed and bound by Cromwell Press, Trowbridge, Wiltshire

NOTE: The material contained in this book is set out in good faith for general guidance and no liability
can be accepted for loss or expense incurred as a result of relying in particular circumstances on
statements made in the book. The laws and regulations are complex and liable to change, and readers
should check the current position with the relevant authorities before making personal arrangements.

Contents

List of Illustrations

Preface
to the Fifth Edition

'The best country in the world in which to live.' That's how the United Nations referred to Canada. That must have something to do with why so many people from all over the world fancy making it their home. In the last ten years an average of 221,000 people per year have immigrated to Canada. This doesn't include those who go on working holidays staying for months or even years. The United Nations were referring to the standard of living, but Canada's attraction is more than that. If you are one of the many who find the Canadian lifestyle appealing, I hope that this book will help you to make your dream a reality.

The idea of working in Canada – whether in the short, the medium or the long term – is an attractive prospect for many. Often those who visit Canada on holiday find the way of life very appealing; others respond to the challenge of the 'wide open spaces'. Certainly Canada is large and varied enough to offer an enormous range of opportunities – from the cosmopolitan outlook of cities such as Toronto and Vancouver to the slower and yet equally challenging lifestyle found in remote areas.

Anyone who is thinking of working in Canada needs to consider carefully many aspects – it's a very big country and there can be, quite literally, a world of difference between city and town, east and west, mountain and prairie. In this book those differences are made clear and you will find out what opportunities are available and where. More importantly, you will be led step by step through the whole process of achieving Employment Authorisation, finding the job you want and landing that job.

I have tried to include as much information as possible to help you in your venture. One of the problems with such a vast country is that there is an equally vast amount of contacts. Where these have been too many to list I have indicated where the information can be found. Just about all the references I have given should be easy to find, either when you begin your job search here at home or when you continue it in Canada.

The section on Immigration is a pretty big one, as really that is the key to the whole procedure. Without Employment Authorisation you simply will not be able to work in Canada. So wade your way through the information there. I hope it will help you to get that magic visa! And remember that approximately 90 per cent of all Skilled Worker applications are successful. I hope you will be, too.

There are addresses throughout the book, as well as in the Useful Addresses section at the back. Often these are just a small sample of the services available. You will come across many more.

Needless to say, there have been some changes since I last updated this book in 2004. I have tried to incorporate as much new information as possible. In particular, the massive growth of the Internet has changed the playing field. In the last edition I mentioned that access to the Internet, although not essential, would make your search for information and contacts so much quicker. Of course there is still a wealth of material available in books, directories and other publications, but I am now inclined to say that Internet access will make your task a lot easier and more productive. There is information on the net that simply does not appear elsewhere and, in most cases, it is the most up-to-date source. Fortunately, if you don't use the net at home it is not a problem as all you need do is visit any reasonably sized library where you can use public access computers and gain Internet connection. There is usually a very small fee to pay and, should you need assistance or advice, the librarians are trained in computer use and are there to help. I have included more relevant website addresses in the Useful Addresses section, but really these are only the tip of the iceberg. You're bound to come across even more informative sites as you search.

I would like to thank all those who have supplied me with information for this new edition. The folks at *Canada News* have provided invaluable assistance. Their magazine is a source of information about Canadian employment and lifestyle that you should definitely not be without.

In previous editions I was wary of painting too rosy a picture of employment prospects and living conditions in Canada. This is still the case, although as things stand currently it is very difficult not to be very enthusiastic. Canada is enjoying the strongest growth in living standards of all G7 countries, as well as boasting the best employment record. But do be aware that, as with all things, economies change. Your best bet is to keep yourself up to date with current trends. There's plenty of information in this book about how to do just that. The opportunities are there if you have the right skills and know where to look.

I hope you enjoy your Canadian adventure and wish you the very best of luck.

Valerie Gerrard

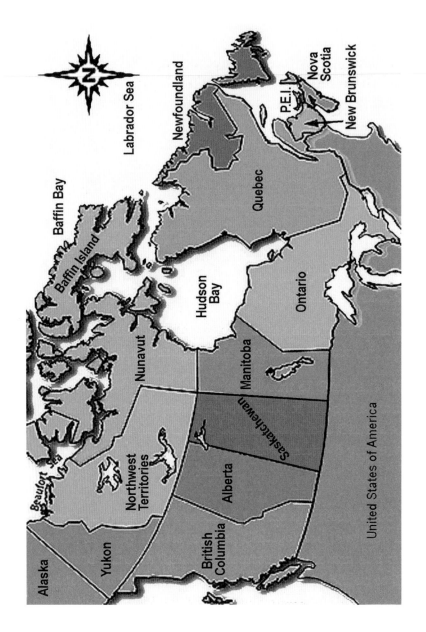

Fig. 1. Map of Canada.

$$\boxed{1}$$

Deciding to Work in Canada

LEARNING ABOUT THE COUNTRY

If you are considering working in Canada you probably know something about the country already. This section will help reinforce your knowledge.

Size and population

Canada covers 9,970,610 square km, which is about the size of all of Europe. Since the dissolution of the USSR Canada is the largest country in the world. With over 32 million inhabitants it ranks twenty-eighth in the world in terms of population. So we really are talking land of the wide open spaces!

It is worth noting, however, that approximately 77 per cent of those 32 million live in the major towns and cities, and 31 per cent of those are in the three major cities of Toronto, Montreal and Vancouver. (See Figure 2 for details of population distribution by provinces and territories.)

Climate

It is impossible to give an overall view of the climate of this vast country which stretches from the temperate southern area bordering on the United States to the frozen wastes of the Arctic Circle. Temperatures can range from a summer daytime high of 35°C in some southern areas to daytime winter lows of −25°C in the far north.

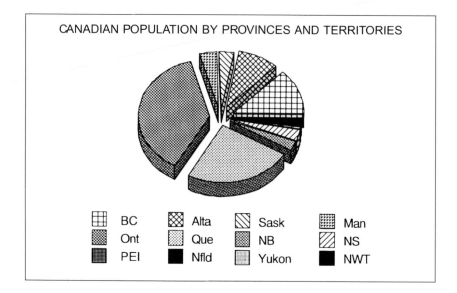

Fig. 2. Canadian population percentage distribution.

Understanding government structure

If you are coming from Britain you will find the Canadian system of government very familiar. It is based on the British model and has a constitutional monarchy. The Governor General of Canada represents the Queen, the Senate is similar to the UK House of Lords and the main body of government is an elected House of Commons.

What can be confusing for the newcomer is the allocation of power between the **federal** and the **provincial governments**. Canada comprises 10 **provinces** and three **territories**, each of which has its own autonomous provincial government responsible for education, local taxes, transportation, aspects of health care, etc. The federal government, as described above, deals with national issues such as foreign policy, national taxation and the economy.

UNDERSTANDING THE PEOPLE

Knowing about multiculturalism

The vast size and varying environments within Canada affect the people and their attitudes. But perhaps the most influential factor is multiculturalism. Canada is officially proud of its multicultural heritage and although not everyone may share this sentiment, most Canadians have, by necessity, a healthy and open attitude towards those from diverse cultures.

This attitude is necessary because of the great number of people from many countries who have made Canada their home over the years. Over 11 million Canadians have some ethnic origin other than British or French, including German, Italian, Ukrainian, Dutch, Polish, Chinese, South Asian, Jewish, Caribbean, Portuguese and Scandinavian. Indeed, one in every six Canadians in their 20s is an immigrant, while one in every five has at least one parent who is an immigrant.

Speaking the language

As you are probably aware, there are two official languages in Canada: English and French. Official forms and consumer goods produced in Canada appear with both languages on them. So, if nothing else, English speakers will soon learn the French for 'taxable allowance', 'flakes of corn', and 'free gift inside'.

In fact, 16 per cent of Canadians are bilingual, with 16 million having English as their mother tongue and 6.5 million claiming French as their first language. Interestingly, the third most common language is Chinese.

You will not find it necessary to be bilingual in most parts of Canada, although it would probably be foolish to try to get a job in the Province of Quebec without excellent written and spoken French. No matter where you choose to work, though, you will need to have a good grasp of English and French if you are aiming for any sort of federal government job.

Not to be confused with...
The United States! If you really want to rile a Canadian, call him an American or say that you can't see much difference between the two countries. There are huge differences: in attitude, culture and politics. And it is true that Canadians are healthier, live longer, spend more on health care and have lower rates of chronic disease than their neighbours to the south.

FINDING OUT ABOUT THE LIFESTYLE
The United Nations declared Canada 'the best country in the world in which to live' in terms of lifestyle. Why? Certainly the standard of living, which we will look at more closely, has a lot to do with it, but perhaps it is more the *style* of living that makes Canada so appealing.

Taking sport seriously
As indicated above, Canada has a great deal of room for manoeuvre and that in itself is a major attraction. It also accounts for the predominantly outdoor nature of the Canadian lifestyle. Sport plays a major part in most people's lives, and it's not just hockey! (Although almost 500,000 Canadian youngsters participate in organised hockey leagues.) All types of team sports such as baseball, soccer, tennis and rugby are popular, as are the more individual recreations like skiing, skating, sailing,

Economic indicators	Change from 4th quarter 2004	Change from previous year
Gross domestic product	1%	6.3%
Real gross domestic product	0.6%	3.3%
Personal disposable income	0.3%	3.6%

Fig. 3. Canada economic indicators.

windsurfing, etc. The varied climate leads to a great diversity in the types of recreation available. There is no doubt that Canadians consider sports of all types an integral part of their lives.

The announcement that Vancouver will be host city for the 2010 Winter Olympics was big news, both for sport and for the economy. Vancouver will be home to the Olympic Village and stadium whilst the ski resort of Whistler, further north, will accommodate the skiing and sliding events. With 1.8 million tickets available, this is a huge boon to tourism. Many other industries, including construction and retail, will inevitably benefit.

Recognising the arts
There is a great interest in the arts in Canada. Stratford, Ontario, is home to a Shakespearean company of worldwide repute. Both Vancouver and Montreal have prestigious symphony orchestras. Opera lovers are well served by the Vancouver Opera Association, the Canadian Opera Company and others. Montreal's annual jazz festival is world-renowned. Canada boasts three large ballet companies – the Royal Winnipeg Ballet, Les Grands Ballets Canadiens and the National Ballet of Canada – which perform

regularly on the international circuit to great acclaim. In the world of television and cinema, Canada's profile has grown much stronger of late. Always respected for producing 'artistic' movies, Canadian cinematographers are enjoying increasing involvement in Hollywood productions, with Vancouver and Toronto vying for the title of 'Hollywood of the North'.

Many cities are home to theatre companies, orchestras, opera groups and art galleries of high standard. In the more remote areas such cultural advantages become thinner on the ground but are generally not ignored.

Attitudes to work

Any observation on a country's attitude to work will be a generalisation, and Canada's vast size and multiculturalism make any such generalisation suspect. However, it would be true to say that the Canadian attitude to work is informal and perhaps less tense than in, say, America or parts of Europe. That is not to say that Canadians do not work hard or have high ambitions, but rather that work is generally seen as only a part (albeit a very important part) of the fabric of life.

Looking at the economy

It's pretty much impossible to keep this information up to date, as the world economy is in a constant state of change. However, I am pleased to say that the good news of continued economic growth in Canada that I reported in the fourth edition of this book published in 2004 continues. Canada currently has one of the world's strongest economies and the future is looking very bright with an expected growth of 3.2 per cent in 2005.

As of July 2005, the unemployment rate stood at 6.8 per cent which, according to Statistics Canada (StatsCan), is 'among the lowest in almost three decades'. Inflation is currently at 1.7 per cent and the primary interest rate is 4.25 per cent.

The ever-changing nature of the world economy means it is inevitable that the above information will change. Fortunately, it's not difficult to get recent data. Statistics Canada release regular updates. These are available at most libraries and from the website www.statcan.ca/ Also, the monthly magazine *Canada News* will keep you informed of current trends.

INVESTIGATING THE STANDARD OF LIVING

Canadians enjoy one of the highest living standards in the world: approximately 99 per cent of families have a colour television and 75 per cent own at least one car; 2.7 per cent of these have two or more. Since 1997, Canada has ranked first amongst all the G7 Countries (the world's richest nations – France, the United States, Britain, Germany, Japan, Italy and Canada) for growth in living standards. It also has the best employment record of all those nations. Although, as mentioned above, there are always economic fluctuations, Canada has a very healthy standard of living which looks set to continue.

Reckoning the cost of living

The price of consumer goods tends to be lower than in the UK. Electrical appliances and computers are usually available at lower prices and in most areas fresh food is cheaper. Certain items such as petrol are considerably less expensive. Figure 4 gives the latest consumer price index for Canada, and Figure 5 gives statistics on average expenditure.

	June 2004	June 2005	% change
All items	125.1	127.2	1.7
Food	125.6	128.9	2.6
Shelter	120.3	123.8	2.9
Household operations and furnishings	115.0	115.7	0.6
Clothing and footwear	101.9	101.3	−0.6
Transportation	147.1	149.7	1.8
Health and personal care	119.1	121.1	1.7
Recreation, education and reading	128.4	127.8	−0.5
Alcoholic beverages and tobacco products	144.0	147.7	2.6

Fig. 4. Consumer price index. Source: Statistics Canada 2005.

AVERAGE EXPENDITURE PER HOUSEHOLD	
Item	Annual expenditure ($ Cdn)
Food	6,791
Shelter	11,584
Household operation	2,870
Household furnishings and equipment	1,751
Clothing	2,436
Transportation	8,353
Health care	1,588
Personal care	834
Recreation	3,591
Reading materials and other printed matter	283
Education	1,007
Tobacco products and alcoholic beverages	1,489
Games of chance (net amount)	272
Miscellaneous	904
Personal income taxes	12,370
Personal insurance premiums and pension contributions	3,505
Gifts of money and contributions	1,522

Fig. 5. Average household expenditure. Source: Statistics Canada 2005.

AVERAGE HOUSE PRICES BY PROVINCE (Cdn $)	
Province	Average price
British Columbia	303,333
Alberta	216,794
Saskatchewan	121,984
Manitoba	139,195
Ontario	252,913
Quebec	188,244
New Brunswick	123,732
Prince Edward Island	114,223
Nova Scotia	157,524
Newfoundland and Labrador	140,598

Fig. 6. Guide to Canadian House prices by province.

Assessing house prices

The price of housing varies enormously across Canada, with Montreal, Toronto and Vancouver being the most expensive cities in which to buy a home. The least expensive house prices are in Saskatchewan and Manitoba. See Figure 6, which is a guide to house prices on a province-by-province basis. Prices are in Canadian dollars. Do remember that this table is just a rough guide, as the housing market is constantly changing. More up-to-date information can be obtained from real estate agents in the areas of interest (see Canadian *Yellow Pages* in main libraries) or from the Internet. A multiple listing service website is available at www.mls.ca To give a general idea, the average price of a house in Canada is around $236,000. That's about £110,000. This works out at roughly 30 per cent of average household income. Prices are expected to rise at an annual rate of 3.2 per cent.

Interest rates are currently fairly low. There are several different kinds of mortgages available and for varying periods. Needless to say, the rates do fluctuate but currently the five-year fixed-rate mortgage is about 5.8% and a five-year variable mortgage approximately 4.2%. Again, this is a guideline only and you can get up-to-date figures from real estate agents, relocation experts and various sites on the Internet, such as www.ldcanadatrust.com/mortgages/numbers. It is worth remembering that several provinces also have a land transfer or property tax. If you're looking for a house in BC, Manitoba, Ontario, Quebec or Nova Scotia this can add one to five per cent to the cost of the property.

CONSULTING THE FAMILY

You may find all these facts and figures rather dry, but it really is worth knowing what you are letting yourself in for before you start the sometimes complicated and lengthy process of getting a permit to work in Canada and finding a suitable job. Which leads us to the last part of this chapter: consulting the family. Just a few more facts and figures!

Generally, Canada is a 'family' sort of place. As shown above, recreational facilities are excellent and there is a broad cultural heritage to draw on. Most people have no trouble adapting to what is recognised as a pleasant and easy-going lifestyle.

Going with your spouse

Realistically, the accompanying partner is most likely to be female so it is worth looking at the role of women in Canada. You will find little difference between the Canadian and the British attitude towards women. The predominant family type is now the dual earner couple, with 60 per cent of women in the labour force.

There is still some wage disparity, with women earning on average 72 per cent of what men make for full-time work despite the fact that equal pay for equal work laws have been in place for over a decade.

Women make up 45 per cent of the labour force and 30 per cent of all self-employed persons.

All jurisdictions give the statutory right to maternity leave (usually 17 weeks unpaid and 37 weeks parental leave). This is in addition to the Federal Unemployment Insurance Scheme which gives 15 weeks of maternity benefits.

Taking your children
There shouldn't be a great deal of upheaval in terms of education. Canada has had to respond to great cultural diversity and many schools have students from 20 or more distinct ethnocultural groups. For example, in Toronto and Vancouver over half the students in elementary and secondary schools can speak languages other than English or French.

Generally, schooling starts at six (although in some areas kindergarten places are available from four onwards) and is compulsory until 16. Most students, however, stay on until at least 18 years of age. This education is free. Bear in mind that there is no national system – each province is responsible for its own arrangements. For further details contact:

The Canadian School Boards Association
340 Laurier Avenue West

PO Box 2095
Ottawa, ON KIP 5W3
email: admin@cdnsba.org

The School Solution is a guide to Canada's schools which includes information on pre-school programmes, elementary and secondary education, out of school activities and curriculum details. It is obtainable from:

Canada Information Services
Suite 421, 253 College St
Toronto, ON M5T 1R5

This is, by the way, a good source for other information about Canada. They will send a list of other publications available with your order form.

Many independent schools are also available. For more information contact:

Canadian Association of Independent Schools
PO Box 820
Lakefield, ON K0L 2H0
email: admin@cais.ca

University and post-secondary education is widely available and, again, varies from province to province. Once you have an idea of what area of Canada you will relocate to you can write for guidance to:

The Canadian Society for the Study of Higher Education
c/o Center for Higher Education Research & Development
University of Manitoba
2205 Sinnott Bldg
70 Dysart Rd
Winnipeg, MB R3T2 N2
email: rzeszute@ms.umanitoba.ca

The International Education Office for each province can provide information on courses available. See Useful Addresses for contact details.

You can also obtain a comprehensive guide to Canadian universities entitled *U-Choose – A Guide to Canadian Universities* from:

Moving To Magazines Ltd
178 Main St
Unionville, Ontario L3R 2G9
Fax: (905) 479 1286
email: info@movingto.com
www.movingto.com

This guide lists approximately 60 universities, and outlines admission requirements, courses/programmes offered, fees, housing/residence, library resources, athletic programmes and facilities, etc. I should add that their website (see above) is very well worth a visit. You can request all sorts of free information from them.

Other organisations which can provide information on Canadian education include:

Youth and Student Information
Association of Student Councils
171 College St
Toronto, ON M5T 1PZ

Canadian Bureau for International Education
ste1550, 220 Laurier Ave
Ottawa, ON K1P 5Z9
email: info@cbie.ca

Additionally, the International Education offices of each province are listed in Useful Addresses.

Agreeing your plans
Finally, it cannot be stressed enough that all members of your family who are going to accompany you must be considered. They are going to have to live there too, and while you may be looking forward to spending your leisure time shushing down the slopes with your ski-mad son, your wife may be allergic to snow and your daughter may have a fear of heights! Be sure to talk it over with everyone concerned and make sure they have as many facts as possible. It is really worth taking the time to study the very different areas of Canada. There is a great deal of province-specific information available. Each province and most of the major cities have informative websites on the Internet. The various provincial tourist boards can send you very useful information that will give everybody a good idea of what they are heading for. See the address section at the end of this book for a list of tourist board offices.

CHECKLIST

◆ Canada is committed to multiculturalism. Over 11 million Canadians have some ethnic origin other than British or French.

◆ Federal government is run along very similar lines to that in Britain. Be aware of the importance of the provincial governments, which control education, local taxes and other areas.

◆ The United Nations declared Canada 'the best country in the world in which to live'.

◆ There is a strong emphasis on outdoor activities and sport.

◆ The Canadian attitude to work may be more 'laid back' than you are used to.

◆ The national economy fluctuates in line with global events. Check Statistics Canada updates in major libraries and at their website www.statcan.ca/

◆ Educational facilities are good and similar to those in Britain. They do, however, vary from province to province.

◆ Canada is *not* to be confused with the United States! Canadians do not appreciate what they consider to be an unflattering comparison.

CASE STUDIES

Let's take a look at three people who are thinking about moving to, and working in, Canada. Each has different expectations and priorities. We will consider their individual needs, the problems they might encounter and how these difficulties can be resolved.

Samantha Curry seeks a complete change

Samantha is looking for a complete change of lifestyle. She is bored with her life in Britain and her job as a dietitian at the local hospital. She visited Vancouver on holiday last year and fell in love with the lifestyle there. She is 24 years old and single, living at home with her widowed mother. Sam doesn't intend to move to Canada for the rest of her life, but would like to try it for a few years.

Having already visited Canada, Samantha has a fairly good, if perhaps superficial, idea of the lifestyle there. She is determined that she wants to live and work in Canada for a few years but her widowed mother, whose impression of Canada is one of Eskimos and frozen wastes, is concerned.

Samantha shows her mother some of the information she has already gathered about Canada, pointing out that almost 80 per cent of Canadians live in major towns and cities.

'The United Nations named Canada the best place in the world to live. They can't have been talking about living in igloos, can they?' Sam points out.

Sam's mother is a bit more comfortable with the idea, but still feels she needs to know a lot more before she will be happy about it.

George Robins wants to further his career

A 38-year-old electronics engineer, George has felt for some time that his career has not been progressing as he would wish. He wants to work in a more forward-looking country, but does not fancy moving himself, his wife and two young children to the United States. He sees Canada as the ideal compromise. Although nervous about the move, his family supports his ambition and is willing to take up a new life in Canada.

George gathers the family together for a discussion. His wife is concerned about how they will fit in.

'Won't they think of us as foreign?' she wonders. 'And we don't speak French.'

George explains the multicultural aspect of Canadian life. His wife is surprised to learn that people of so many nationalities make their home there.

'And French is only one of the official languages,' George points out. 'In most parts you don't need it at all.'

George and his family realise that they have quite a bit still to learn about life in Canada and decide to get some books from the library. There the librarian tells them that the Internet contains a wealth of information about Canada and suggests a few sites to start off with, such as www.canada.org.uk Back home, the family is able to learn a great deal more about the very different areas of Canada and begins to get quite excited about the proposed move.

Lucy Martin thinks the grass may be greener

Lucy is in her first year of a degree course in environmental studies at East Anglia University. After two years of A levels and then going straight to university, she badly feels the need for a break.

A friend mentions the BUNAC Work Canada programme. He went on it himself a couple of years ago and had a great time. He is now a BUNAC representative at the college.

'But how did you survive?' Lucy asks. 'Did they find jobs for you?'

'It's up to you to find jobs, but they can give you lots of assistance. You can either try to get something before you go or bite the bullet and start looking when you arrive.'

'I think I'd rather find something before I leave,' says Lucy. 'I don't have very much money saved. Just that bit I got when Mum died last year.'

'Didn't you say you had an aunt living in Canada?'

Indeed Lucy's mother was Canadian and her sister still lives in Ottawa. Lucy's friend explains that with a personal sponsor, she will need less funding.

Lucy joins BUNAC and attends a Work Canada Info Session, after which she is very enthusiastic. She tells her friend she has decided to go ahead with the year out.

'Great. You'll have a fantastic time. After all, Canada is the ideal place for someone doing environmental studies.'

'Why?' asks Lucy.

'Well, it's a big place. Bound to have lots of environment.'

Lucy laughs, but is still nervous about the venture.

POINTS TO CONSIDER

1. How do you think your way of life will change when you move to Canada? There are many positive points; can you think of anything which might be a negative factor?

2. How will the multicultural elements of Canadian life affect you? Your family? Would you regard this as a negative or positive feature?

3. Some people who move from Britain to Canada react badly to the vastness of the country and the greatly increased space. Might this prove a problem for you?

4. Do you know anyone who has emigrated to Canada? Could you get in touch with them and find out about their experience? Could they give you any tips?

5. Have you considered the implications of living so far from family and/or friends?

Dealing with Immigration

UNDERSTANDING THE PROCESS

Many factors are involved in your search for a job in Canada: location, duration, the job itself. One thing, however, is essential in all cases. You will have to obtain permission to work in Canada from the Citizenship and Immigration Canada (CIC). For that reason this chapter is a fairly long and detailed one, to give you a complete understanding of the immigration process and how to make your way successfully through it.

Canada's immigration policy is a positive one. The Government is keen for a number of qualified people to enter Canada each year and become a vital part of the Canadian economy. Over the last ten years, an average of 221,000 people have successfully emigrated to Canada each year. However, new rules were introduced in 2002 which made it a bit more difficult to gain an immigrant visa (or Permanent Resident status as it is now known). Consequently, that year the total number of immigrants to Canada dropped, although the figure was still nearing 230,000. Obviously the changes were successful because in 2004 the total number of immigrants admitted into Canada rose to a whopping 235,808, a 7 per cent increase from 2003. This constitutes the seventh highest number of successful immigrants since records began in 1860 and the second highest since 1993. The number of immigrants arriving from the UK rose by 17 per cent to 6,056, which is the highest number for more than a decade. The UK ranks currently as Canada's seventh most popular host country.

This chapter will look in detail at the different routes of entry into Canada. However, a word of warning and it's a big one – *look out for changes.* To give an idea of just how true that statement is, I had just about finished the updates to this book's previous 2004 edition, incorporating all the new rules brought in during 2002 when the latest copy of *Canada News* popped through my door informing me that the Canadian government had just announced significant changes to the procedure. In this case it was good news, making it easier to qualify as a skilled worker. Fortunately for me, as I prepare this fifth edition, I see that not a lot of changes have occurred between then and now. But the lesson has been learned – *look out for changes.*

Fortunately there are plenty of sources to help you do just that. A subscription to *Canada News* gives you monthly updates and there is information available on the Internet too. The CIC website includes a page (www.cic.gc.ca/irpa_lipr) where you can see any changes to immigration and citizenship legislation pretty much as they happen. This page, with a link to frequently asked questions, together with a less technical page (www.cic.gc.ca/english/irpa/facts.html) will help you keep up to date. Check out the Canada News on-line site (canadanews.co.uk) for all the latest.

So, use the information in this chapter as a guideline but – *look out for changes!*

Generally, you stand a good chance of getting an immigrant visa if:

◆ You have a good education.

◆ Your employment skills are applicable to the Canadian labour market.

◆ You have the necessary language and communications skills (English and/or French).

◆ You are of good character.

◆ You are in good health.

◆ You have sufficient funds to support yourself (and your family, if applicable) when settling in Canada.

Three visa routes

There are three basic routes via which immigrants are admitted to Canada:

1. **Family class**. A sponsored immigration programme designed to reunite families.

2. **Refugee and Humanitarian Class**.

3. **Independent Class**. This is the one we will look at in detail. It includes skilled workers, entrepreneurs, investors and self-employed persons.

Within the Independent Class there are four different types of applicant to consider:

1. A skilled worker requesting permanent status.

2. A temporary, vacation or exchange worker.

3. An entrepreneur or business person intending to start or invest in a business in Canada.

4. Provincial nominee.

The vast majority will gain their permits via the first route.

Starting the process

Although the process can appear complicated it is in fact fairly simple, being based on a points system. Further on in this chapter we will look at how cases are assessed and you will be able to work out for yourself what your points total is likely to be.

In many cases the application will be straightforward and, with the help of this book and the information you will receive from the Canadian High Commission, you will be able to complete the process without any other assistance. Once you have filled in all the forms and provided all the information required, the Canadian High Commission acknowledges your application. After that it's a bit of a waiting game. Be prepared to be patient as the recently reported processing times for all Permanent Resident applications are:

Within 13 months	Within 21 months	Within 31 months	Within 38 months
30%	50%	70%	80%

Be aware that it can take even longer. In the case of skilled workers, reported times are up to 41 months and for Business immigrant applications up to 47 months. Which, admittedly, sounds a bit discouraging for independent class applicants. It might help to know that you can check up on the status of your application on-line at any time. You can call the Automated Voice Request Service (AVRES) on 020 7258 6699. Or, easier still, you can become an 'e-client' and get updates on-line. Simply go to the Canadian Immigration homepage (www.cic.gc.ca) and click on the 'On-line services' button. This will take you to the e-client facility where application progress information is updated weekly. Make sure you have the following to hand:

◆ a copy of your application;

◆ your financial receipt(s) (IMM 5401); or

◆ any letter or official document issued to you by the CIC

whilst your application is being processed.

You (and accompanying family members) will be required to be examined by a medical practitioner designated by Canadian Immigration.

As the process continues you will be advised of any queries or problems that may require further processing. If you do not meet requirements you will be given a written explanation.

If you are applying for a temporary work permit or study permit, the process takes much less time. According to CIC statistics, 91 per cent of temporary work permit applications are completed within 28 days and 87 per cent of study permits within 28 days.

Spotting likely difficulties

The areas that can cause difficulties include criminal convictions, lack of training and health problems. There are agencies and firms which may be able to help you overcome those obstacles, and these are dealt with in detail later in this chapter.

There is one more wrinkle. If you are intending to immigrate to Quebec the process is slightly different. That, too, will be outlined in this chapter.

MEETING THE REQUIREMENTS

Applying as a skilled worker requesting permanent resident status

The majority of applicants will fall into this category. This category applies to you if you are not:

◆ aiming for a temporary permit or

◆ intending to start a business in Canada.

There are three steps to finding out if you qualify in this category:

◆ You must meet the minimum work experience requirements.

◆ You will need to prove that you have sufficient funds for resettlement.

◆ You must gain sufficient points to pass six selection factors.

Take each step one by one – less daunting that way.

Assessing work experience

This is probably the most important step, as you will need to have relevant experience in an occupation on the National Occupations Classification (NOC) list. This is a minimum requirement, so if your occupation is not shown on the list you should probably leap straight to the last section of this chapter and consider engaging the services of an immigration consultant.

The CIC website has a user-friendly page (www.cic.gc.ca/english/ skilled/qual-2.html) to help you determine if your occupation qualifies. You can get a fairly good idea if you qualify by checking out the NOC list in Appendix 1, but I would definitely recommend going to the website for the fullest and most up-to-date information. Note that there is also a list of restricted occupations. If your only work experience falls under any of these, your application will automatically be rejected. The good news is that, currently, there are no restricted occupations, but you should check this on the website too.

If you don't find your occupation on the NOC list, it is worth thinking about checking for any other work experience you have, as you may qualify under another heading. For example, a plumber might quality as a pipe fitter. The relevant work experience must have taken place in the ten years before your application.

Once you've determined that you meet the minimum requirement, it's time to move on to the next step.

Proving sufficient funds for resettlement
The Canadian government does not provide any financial support for newly immigrated skilled workers. You must prove that you have sufficient funds to support your family for the first six months you are in Canada. The following shows the minimum amounts required. However, it would be very wise to do a bit of research into the cost of living and wages in the area of Canada you are headed for.

Note that you do not have to prove you have these funds if you have pre-arranged employment in Canada.

Number in family	Minimum funds required (C$)
1	9,897
2	12,372
3	15,387
4	18,626
5	20,821
6	23,015
7 or more	25,210

Passing the selection factors

In October 2003, the passing number of points for the selection grid was lowered from 75 to 67. The Canadian Immigration Minister, in response to warnings from the immigration industry, recognised that the higher mark was limiting the number of much-needed migrants to Canada.

There are six elements to the selection factor. These are education, proficiency in one or both of Canada's official languages (English and French), work experience, age, arranged employment (where applicable) and adaptability. It's a fairly long list, but not really complicated if you go through it point by point. The following shows the six factors and the points available in each. Read the detailed explanations and then go to Figure 9 for a simple worksheet on which you can tally your points. And do remember the CIC website listed above – it really is very helpful and easy to manoeuvre around.

Education

Note that the full-time or full-time equivalent study requirement refers to total number of years in full-time study (or equivalent). If you have completed less than the number of years stated you must decrease points accordingly. For example, if you have a PhD but only 15 years of study, you get 22, rather than 25 points.

Maximum points available 25

University degrees

PhD or Masters AND at least 17 years full-time or full-time equivalent study	25
Two or more university degrees at Bachelor level AND at least 15 years full-time or full-time equivalent study	22
Two-year university degree at Bachelor level AND at least 14 years full-time or full-time equivalent study	20
One-year university degree at Bachelor level AND at least 13 years full-time or full-time equivalent study	15

Trade or non-university certificate or diploma

Three-year diploma, trade certificate or apprenticeship AND at least 15 years of full-time or full-time equivalent study	22
Two-year diploma, trade certificate or apprenticeship AND at least 14 years of full-time or full-time equivalent study	20
One-year diploma, trade certificate or apprenticeship AND at least 13 years of full-time or full-time equivalent study	15
One-year diploma, trade certificate or apprenticeship AND at least 12 years of full-time or full-time equivalent study	12
Secondary School Educational Credential	5

Language

Score separately for Speaking, Reading, Listening and Writing – e.g. high proficiency in all four categories for first language equals a maximum of 16 points. Note, however, that you can only claim a maximum of two points for basic level proficiency.

Maximum points available 24

Proficiency in First Language

High	4
Moderate	2
Basic	1
None	0

Proficiency in Second Language

If you are claiming proficiency in a language other than your native tongue you will be required to provide proof. A language test by an approved organisation is the preferred method.

High	2
Moderate	2
Basic	1 to 2
None	0

Work experience

Experience must have been gained during the ten years previous to your application. Consult the National Occupations Classification list (NOC) to find out if your occupation is eligible.

Maximum points available 21

One year	15
Two years	17
Three years	19
Four years	21

Age

Maximum points available 10

21–49	10

then deduct two points for every year below 21 and above 49

Arranged employment

This must be confirmed by Human Resources and Skills Development Canada (HRSDC).

Maximum points available 10

An HRSDC confirmed offer of permanent employment   10

Applicants from within Canada holding a temporary work
  permit that is validated by the HRSDC, or exempt from
  HRSDC validation under international agreements   10

Adaptability

Maximum points available 10

Spouse's education (includes common law partners):

◆ PhD or Masters degree AND at least 17 years of full-time
  equivalent studies   5
◆ Two or three-year diploma, trade certificate, apprenticeship,
  or university degree AND at least 14 years of full-time or
  full-time equivalent studies   4
◆ One-year diploma, trade certificate, apprenticeship, or
  university degree AND at least 12 years of full-time or
  full-time equivalent studies   3
◆ Secondary School Educational Credential   0

Minimum one year full-time authorised work in Canada
  (applies to principal applicant or accompanying spouse/
  common law partner)   5
Minimum two years authorised full-time post-secondary study
  in Canada (applies to principal applicant or accompanying
  spouse/common law partner)   5
Points received under the Arranged Employer factor   5
Family relationship in Canada (applies to principal applicant
  or accompanying spouse/common law partner)   5

Your professional qualifications may not be acceptable as such in the Canadian labour market. You can visit a reference library and consult the *Canadian Almanac & Directory*. There you will find relevant professional organisations in Canada which will be able to advise you whether your qualifications are suitable. Alternatively you could contact:

> The Canadian Information Centre for International Credentials
> 95 St. Clair West, Suite 1106
> Toronto, ON M4V 1N6
> Tel: (416) 962 9725
> Fax: (416) 682 2800
> website: www.cicic.ca/

Follow the website to www.cicic.ca/casinca.stm for more information on credential evaluation services. The web page contains details of the provincial evaluation services as well as three private services that are well regarded.

Additionally, there are Provincial assessment services who, for a fee, will assess academic credentials. (Contact details can be found in the Useful Addresses section at the back of the book.) They will advise how your education compares with educational standards in that particular province and this may help in your job search.

Assessing your score

What you are aiming for is a score of at least 67 points. If that is not achieved, the application is refused. There really is no point in applying if you do not come into that range. Bear in mind that the figure you have come up with is still only an estimate, but at least lets you know if you are in the ballpark.

CASE STUDY

Samantha is quietly confident

Samantha has contacted the Canadian High Commission and now
has all the forms she will need to fill in. Initially, she thought she
would apply for a temporary work permit, as she only wants to
go to Canada for a few years, but she soon realises that her best
route is to go for Permanent Resident status. Most temporary
permits are only valid for a few months.

Working out her points for herself, Samantha is pleased to
estimate them at 73. As a minimum score of 67 is needed, she is
fairly confident and goes ahead with her application.

Samantha's points

Samantha is a qualified nutritionist – an occupation which
appears on the National Occupations Classification List. This is
essential.

	Points
◆ Education (BSc in Nutrition)	20
◆ Language	
fluent English	16
good A level French	8
◆ Work experience (three years)	19
◆ Age (24)	10
◆ Arranged employment	0
◆ Adaptability	0
◆ Samantha's self-assessed total	73

Provincial Nominee Programme

This is a fairly recent scheme which now plays a major part in helping would-be immigrants under the Skilled Worker Category. Most provinces are now participating in the programme. You will see below which are on board. You need first of all to apply directly to the province you are interested in settling in. They will assess your application from two angles – the first is their immigration needs and the second is your genuine intention to settle in that area. If you choose this route you need to first complete the provincial nomination process, then apply to CIC. Provincial nominees are not assessed on the six selection factors applied to Skilled Worker applicants. So if you can't make the magic 67 mark on the immigration points system, this can be a viable alternative. The other big plus is that it could significantly reduce the amount of time you wait to hear of the success of your Permanent Resident application. The Canadian High Commission say that, at the moment, they are processing PNP applications in six to nine months.

Basically, the programme allows participating provincial governments to choose a limited number of immigrants to meet local demand. These applicants are looked on very favourably by immigration officials. The aim of the programme is to increase the skilled workforce in areas where demand is greater than resources. It is definitely a route worth looking into.

Each participating province has a different programme structure and requirements:

Alberta – The scheme here is very much employer-driven in that employers present their needs to the programme, demonstrating that they conform to the following criteria:

- the position can't be filled by a Canadian resident
- they are offering full-time permanent work in Alberta
- the job is being offered to an individual with the required qualifications
- the package meets provincial employment and wage standards
- there is no conflict with existing collective bargaining arrangements.

Potential employees can apply if they:

- have been recruited by a pre-approved Alberta employer
- have a valid job offer.

British Columbia – The programme is targeted to highly skilled immigrants needed to fill critical labour shortages. The prospective employer makes the application. There are three categories:

- strategic occupations – for skilled workers with a guaranteed job offer who are qualified in selected occupations. This would include registered nurses, skilled workers and international students.
- business skills – for individuals with the necessary skills and resources to start a business in BC.
- projects – this category includes managers, employees or business owners who are essential to the success of an economic project(s).

The Manitoba PNP selects skilled workers who will make a positive contribution to the provincial economy. Basic requirements for skilled workers applying for this programme are:

- sufficient training and work experience
- sufficient language ability to begin working soon after arrival
- settlement supports in Manitoba to assist you upon your arrival.

New Brunswick has a two-tier programme. Skilled workers are required to have a guaranteed job offer for permanent and full-time employment consistent with their education, training and experience. The requirements for the Business applicant are:

- previous successful management experience as a senior executive and/or business owner
- skills must be relevant to the business you intend to pursue in New Brunswick
- sufficient funds to finance the first phase of the planned business venture
- sufficient funds to sustain self and dependents for a period of up to two years
- you will participate in the business in an active managerial role.

Newfoundland and Labrador – the process here begins by the province identifying and recruiting immigrants with specialised skills which will benefit the economy. Applicants are assessed on a points system. This applies to skilled workers and business applicants.

Prince Edward Island has a scheme which applies to skilled workers and business applicants. The criteria vary dependent on the nomination class but include:

- an intent to settle in PEI
- proficiency in English or French
- possession of a BA or equivalent
- a guaranteed job offer from a PEI employer for skilled workers.

At the beginning of 2005, the province of Saskatchewan launched a revised PNP which will significantly increase openings for PNP applicants in that province. The revised programme allows foreign skilled workers to be nominated for about 45 per cent of jobs in Saskatchewan, well above the 2 per cent of jobs covered under the old guidelines.

The Yukon is looking for people with a good business background as well as experience in the production and marketing of goods. Applicants must demonstrate the following:

- experience in operating a business
- minimum net worth of C$250,000
- at least one visit to the Yukon within the last three years
- reasonable ability in French or English.

Nova Scotia operates two streams within its PNP. The first is for skilled workers for whom the basic requirements are:

- basic literacy in English or French and English
- minimum Grade 12 education (generally 13 years of education)
- 18 years and over.

The second stream relates to economic development. A privately owned company operating in Nova Scotia can offer a nominee employment in a middle management position for a minimum of six months.

The above gives you a basic idea. If you follow the direct link on the CIC homepage to 'Provincial Nomination' you can see a lot more information, listed by province. In some cases you can even access and download application forms.

Applying as a temporary, exchange or vacation worker

In almost all cases you will require a work permit to work temporarily in Canada. Please note that this is temporary and you must leave Canada when the permit expires. There are some jobs which are exempt from the work permit requirement. The current list is available at www.cic.gc.ca/english/work/exempt-1.html

The procedure for gaining a work permit consists of two steps:

♦ You must have a confirmed job offer, which will have to be verified by Human Resources and Skills Development Canada (HRSDC). They will approve it if they are satisfied that the job cannot be filled by a Canadian resident.
♦ If HRSDC approval is obtained, you then need to apply to CIC for your work permit.

Applying for a student work programme

More than 130,000 foreign students study in Canada each year. If your course of study is less than six months you will not require a student permit. However, for anything longer you will need one and, in any case, it is best to apply for a permit no matter what the length of your course. Circumstances change and with a permit you will be able to apply for renewal from within Canada if necessary. Another important point is that, once in possession of a student permit, you will be allowed to work part-time on campus. Every little bit helps!

You must have a formal acceptance from a Canadian educational institution to apply for a student permit.

BUNAC operates a student exchange programme for those taking a year out from college/university or having a gap year. They will advise you on the visa process. Further details about BUNAC can be found in Chapter 4.

CASE STUDY

Lucy gets helps with her visa

As she hopes to go to Canada as a temporary student worker, Lucy does not follow the same procedure as those who are applying for independent immigrant status. She is delighted to learn that BUNAC will see the application through Canada Immigration.

'You'll need to get your forms in to us as soon as possible, though,' advises her BUNAC counsellor. 'There are only a limited number of places each year and it is essential to get everything to us as soon as possible. Certainly before March.'

Lucy puts together her application and pays her fees to BUNAC. She has been advised that she will be required to provide evidence of sufficient funds to support herself on arrival in Canada. This is proving to be a problem, as she doesn't have much of her small inheritance left.

'You might like to ask your aunt if she will act as a personal sponsor. That way you will only need C$550,' advises BUNAC.

Lucy writes to her aunt in Ottawa and waits for the reply before making her final application.

Applying as a live-in caregiver

Included in this category are nannies and workers qualified to care for the disabled, children with special needs and the elderly. Full details of the Live-in Caregiver programme can be found in Chapter 4.

Obtaining Employment Authorisation

If you have a Canadian job offer (which, as in the case of a permanent resident application, must be certified by a Canada Human Resources Employment Centre) you should apply to the Canadian High Commission for **Employment Authorisation** (a work permit). This is not transferable between jobs. You may be able to obtain Employment Authorisation that allows for swapping jobs, but it is not the norm. In some cases your authorisation may be valid for up to three years.

The key to temporary authorisation is proof that there are no Canadian citizens or landed immigrants available to carry out the job.

Others on exchange visits must also obtain Employment Authorisation, but this will normally be handled by the association or agency arranging the exchange. Exchange teachers should contact The League of Exchange of Commonwealth Teachers. (See Chapter 4 for further information.)

Applying as an entrepreneur or business person intending to start a business in Canada

If you fall within this category your application will be given priority treatment and your chances of success are very good. Known as the **Business Immigration Scheme**, this category is aimed at entrepreneurs, investors and the self-employed. You should contact the Business Immigration Centre at the Canadian High Commission for complete details, but the following will give you a brief outline of how the scheme works.

Entrepreneur category

This applies to someone who is experienced in business, and who intends to buy or establish a business which will create jobs for one or more Canadians and make a significant contribution to the economy. Successful applicants are granted a conditional visa. Within two years of the visa being issued they must establish a business which employs at least one Canadian. You will need to prove that you have sufficient funds to accomplish this. You must be able to prove a net worth of C$300,000.

Investor category

To qualify for the investor category you must have successfully operated, controlled or directed a business or commercial undertaking and have accumulated a net worth of minimum C$800,000. You will then be required to make an investment of at least C$400,000 for five years in Canadian business. Investors have no conditions imposed upon their entry to Canada.

Self-employed category

Finally, within the Business Immigration Scheme is the self-employed person category. This describes someone who intends to purchase or set up a small business in Canada that will create employment for himself. Additionally, the applicant must provide documentary evidence that their intended business will make a significant difference to the economy or cultural life of Canada. Athletes and creative professionals such as writers and performers could come under this category.

Immigration to Quebec

The procedure is much the same but the points awarded for occupation are geared to the opportunities for employment in Quebec.

You can obtain and complete an application form on-line at www.cic.gc.ca/english/skilled/quebec/index.html, where you will also find step-by-step instructions for applying and lots of useful information. If you cannot go on-line, you need to contact the Canadian High Commission in London.

If successful, you will be given a Quebec Selection Certificate. At that point you join up again with the general Canadian immigration system and will need to complete medical and legal assessments. Fees are chargeable for this process. The whole thing takes from six to twelve months.

Universal requirements

There are two factors that apply no matter what category you apply under. If you have a problem with either of these there is not much point in lodging your application without seeking assistance from an immigration consultant or attorney.

Proving your 'good character'

All immigrants must be of 'good character'. This means that if you have a criminal record you are not going to get a visa. And it is up to you to prove your good record. You will have to provide a police certificate/clearance from each country in which you have lived for six months or more in the last ten years. This also applies to all your dependants aged 18 or over.

If you or any of your dependants do have a criminal conviction in the past it is almost certain that your application will be refused. There is one small glimmer of hope, however. In exceptional circumstances those with criminal convictions may be admitted to Canada on the grounds that they have been 'rehabilitated'. You may not apply for approval for rehabilitation until five years after the end of your sentence.

Passing a medical

The other universal criterion is health. You will not be granted a visa if you 'present a health risk or danger to Canadians' or are 'likely to place an excessive demand on Canada's health or social services'. You and all your dependants, whether they are accompanying you to Canada or not, must pass a medical in accordance with the above. This examination must be performed by a physician designated by the Canadian Immigration and Medical Division. You will be given a list of approved doctors when your application reaches that stage, or you can access a list of medical practitioners in your area from the CIC homepage.

APPLYING FOR A VISA

Having established that you are in with a chance, you now need to start the actual process. Remember, though, there is no point in even making the application if it does not look like you will tot up 67 points per the allocations outlined above. That is not to say that you should give up on the whole thing, simply that you will have to do whatever is necessary to increase your points (another year's experience in your job, perhaps, or some additional education). If you think your application is borderline you may decide to get assistance from an immigration consultant or attorney.

Assuming that you are going ahead on your own, here is your step-by-step guide to getting a visa. The following applies if you fall into the first category of skilled worker requesting permanent status. Granting of a temporary visa is usually dependent on a job offer in Canada, and the Business Immigrant Scheme follows a different set of guidelines which are outlined above.

Getting the ball rolling

First write, telephone or visit the **Immigration Division** of the Canadian High Commission in London. They will send you a full set of application forms, including a guide to completing your application. You can also download all the necessary forms from the Canadian government website www.canada.org.uk or www.cic.gc.ca. Just make sure you have plenty of black ink in your printer!

Completing the forms

You will receive:

◆ Application for Permanent Residence in Canada.
◆ Schedule 1 – Background/Declaration.
◆ Additional Family Information.

- Authorisation to Release Information to Designated Individuals.

Now you can start the mammoth task of completing the forms for everybody in your family who is over 18 years of age at the time of the application, regardless of whether they will accompany you to Canada.

The Application Form

Figure 7 shows the Application Form which will give your visa officer the basic information he needs to assess your points. Note that you will need to include photocopies of all your educational, trade and professional qualifications along with evidence of your employment experience. Personal documents such as passports and birth certificates are also required.

Additional Forms

The Additional Family Information form requires even more detailed family information and the Authorisation to Release Information to Designated Individuals confirms that you are agreeable to information regarding your case being made available to your sponsor and/or Canadian representative (if applicable).

Plus, if you are applying under one of the Immigration Programmes, there are even more forms to fill in:

- Schedule 3 – Federal Skilled Workers
- Schedule 4 – Provincial Nominees
- Schedule 5 – Quebec Skilled Workers

Citizenship and Immigration Canada / **Citoyenneté et Immigration Canada**

APPLICATION FOR PERMANENT RESIDENCE IN CANADA

Space reserved for applicant's photo

FOR OFFICE USE ONLY
Office file number (or IMM 1343 Case Label)
Date of receipt stamp at post

Category under which you are applying (see instructions)

☐ Family class   ☐ Refugees outside Canada

☐ Economic class   Other ☐

How many family members (including yourself) are included in this application for permanent residence in Canada?

Language you prefer for:

Correspondence: ☐ English ☐ French

Interview: ☐ English ☐ French Other ☐

1. **Your full name (as shown in your passport or travel document)**

   Family name

   Given name(s)

2. **Your sex** ☐ Male ☐ Female

3. **Your date of birth** Day Month Year

4. **Your place of birth** Town/City

   Country

5. **Your country of citizenship**

6. **Your native language**

7. **Your height** _____ cm OR _____ ft _____ in

8. **Colour of your eyes**

9. **Your current marital status**

   ☐ Never married ☐ Married ☐ Widowed ☐ Legally separated

   ☐ Annulled marriage ☐ Divorced ☐ Common-law

   If you are married or in a common-law relationship, provide the date on which you were married or entered into the common-law relationship   Day Month Year

10. **Have you previously been married or in a common-law relationship?**

    ☐ No ☐ Yes ▶ Give the following details for each previous spouse or partner. If you do not have enough space, provide details on a separate sheet of paper.

    Name of previous spouse or partner

    Date of birth   Day Month Year

    Type of relationship ☐ Marriage ☐ Common-law union

    From Day Month Year   to Day Month Year

11. **Your knowledge of English and French**

    Can you communicate in English? ☐ Yes ☐ No

    Can you communicate in French? ☐ Yes ☐ No

12. **Education**

    How many years of formal education do you have?

    What is your highest level of completed education?

    ☐ No secondary ☐ Bachelor's degree

    ☐ Secondary ☐ Master's degree

    ☐ Trade/Apprenticeship ☐ Ph D

    ☐ Non-university certificate/diploma

13. **Your current occupation**

14. **Your mailing address (include city and country)**

15. **Your residential address, if different from your mailing address**

16. **Your telephone numbers**

    Country code   Area code   Number

    At home ( ) ( )

    Alternative ( ) ( )

17. **Your e-mail address, if applicable**

18. **Details from your passport**

    Passport number

    Country of issue

    Date of expiry   Day Month Year

19. **Your identity card number, if applicable**

20. **Where do you intend to live in Canada?**

    City/Town

    Province

IMM 0008 (06-2002) E
GENERIC

This form is made available by Citizenship and Immigration Canada and is not to be sold to applicants.

(DISPONIBLE EN FRANÇAIS - IMM 0008 F GÉNÉRIQUE)

Canada

Fig. 7. Application form for permanent residence.

Canadian High Commission   **Haut-commissariat du Canada**

Canada

Immigration and Medical Division   Service d'immigration
Macdonald House
38 Grosvenor Street   **UK Fax: 020 7258 6506**
London W1K 4AA   **Outside UK Fax: +44 20 7258 6506**

REQUEST FOR POLICE CERTIFICATES/CLEARANCES

SURNAME:

To Police or Relevant Authorities:

The person who has completed the authorization form below is applying for admission to Canada as a permanent resident. To meet Canadian immigration requirements, each member of his/her family aged 18 years and over requires an original Police Certificate/Clearance of no criminal conviction.

We would ask that the Certificates be provided to the bearer of this letter, who will then forward them to the High Commission. If this is not possible, the Certificates should be sent directly to the High Commission.

Thank you for your co-operation.

The High Commission

TO BE COMPLETED BY APPLICANT

AUTHORIZATION BY VISA APPLICANT
FOR RELEASE OF POLICE AND COURT RECORDS

I hereby authorize the Police or Relevant Authorities in _____(name country) to disclose any details of previous criminal convictions to the Canadian High Commission, London, England, for visa purposes only.

SURNAME:	
GIVEN NAMES:	
MAIDEN OR OTHER SURNAME(S) USED:	
NAME IN ORIGINAL SCRIPT (i.e. Arabic, Chinese etc):	
DATE & PLACE OF BIRTH:	**SEX:**
NATIONALITY:	
ALL ADDRESSES WHILE RESIDENT IN_____(name country)	

DATES	HOME ADDRESS

Fig. 8. Request for police certificates/clearances.

And there's more! You must apply to the Visa Office of your country of residence or nationality. For most people reading this, that will probably be The Canadian High Commission in London. If not, they will be able to advise you of the correct office to apply to, or your can check it out yourself on www.cic.gc.ca/english/ applications/skilled-mission.html Each office has what they call 'visa office specific forms' which you will also need to complete. The most important one of these is the Request for Police Certificates/Clearances (see Figure 8). It is your responsibility to get this completed by the police or relevant authorities in any country in which you lived for six months or longer. This applies to your spouse and any dependent children planning to accompany you to Canada.

Submitting the forms

It is very important to follow the instructions given by Canadian Immigration to the letter. Applications that are incomplete or inaccurate in any way are not given consideration. Use the following checklist to make sure you have included absolutely everything required. Note that in some cases there may be even more that you need to include, but this list should suffice for most applications. Send photocopies only of official documents such as passport, certificates, etc., but be sure to enclose originals of police certificates and language test results (if applicable).

In all cases

- ◆ Application for permanent residence
  - – make sure it's signed!
  - – include photographs as instructed for self and all family members.

- ◆ Schedule 1 Background declaration
  - – for principal applicant, spouse or partner and each dependent child aged over 18.

- ◆ Schedule 3 Economic Classes
  - – passports or travel documents for self, spouse or partner and dependent children.

- ◆ Proof of language proficiency
  - – immigrant summary and supplementary information form in duplicate by all persons over 18
  - – birth certificate for self, spouse and dependent children
  - – work experience documentation for self and spouse or partner
  - – CVs
  - – pay slips and bank statements
  - – organisational chart
  - – notarised employment contracts
  - – letters of reference.

- ◆ Proof of settlement funds.

- ◆ Police certificates and clearances for self, spouse or partner and everyone in the family aged 18 and over.

- ◆ Bank draft in Canadian dollars to cover full immigration fee.

Where applicable
- ◆ Schedule 3: Economic Classes B Federal Skilled Workers
  - – completed by principal applicant.

- ◆ Additional family information
  - – completed by self, spouse or partner and dependent children over 18.

- Authority to release information to designated individuals
  - only if you wish CIC to give information re your application to another person.

- Photocopy and translation of visa for country where you currently live.

- Marriage, final divorce, annulment or separation certificates
  - for self and spouse.

- Proof of common law relationship.

- Death certificate for spouse.

- Adoption papers for adopted children.

- Proof of custody for children aged under 18.

- Proof you have fulfilled custody obligations.
  - if children are not to accompany you.

- Proof of continuous full-time studies of all dependent children aged 22 and over.

- Post-secondary education documents for self and spouse or partner
  - certificates
  - degrees
  - diplomas.

- Professional qualifications certifications for self and spouse or partner.

- Proof of relationship in Canada.

- Arranged employment
  - if currently working in Canada provide photocopy of work permit.

All this is bundled up and sent to the Canadian High Commission. Next you stagger back from the post office and wait to hear. You will receive an acknowledgement and immigration file number within three months. Later in the process you will be required to provide satisfactory medical reports for you, your spouse and children.

Checking and double-checking

Make sure your paperwork is complete. This is sound advice frequently offered by immigration officials. An incomplete application will seriously slow things down, while one containing all the information and documentation required will ensure the fastest processing time. Here are some slips to avoid:

◆ leaving gaps in dates – account for everything

◆ failing to describe your occupation fully – an 'administrative officer' could be almost anything, whereas 'database design and maintenance' indicates a precise occupation

◆ not clearly indicating the occupation you intend to pursue in Canada – points are awarded from the Occupations List, so you must be specific

◆ sending blurred or unclear photocopies

◆ not providing reference letters and/or including letters which fail to describe the job performed

◆ forgetting to include forms for spouse and/or children

◆ sending old photographs – perhaps more flattering, but likely to be rejected.

The Immigration Visa Processing Fee

At the time of writing the fee schedule is:

For skilled workers

	Immigrant Visa Processing Fee C$	Right of Permanent Residence Fee C$
Principal applicant	550	975
Spouse or partner	550	975
Each dependant 22 years and over	550	n/a
Each dependant under 22 years	150	n/a

For entrepreneurs, investors and self-employed

	Immigrant Visa Processing Fee C$	Right of Permanent Residence Fee C$
Principal applicant	1050	975
Spouse or partner	550	975
Each dependent 22 years and over	550	n/a
Each dependent under 22 years	150	n/a

Temporary Residence Permits

Work permit	150	n/a
Study permit	125	n/a

The **Immigrant Visa Processing Fee** is not refundable, regardless of the outcome of your application. The **Right of Permanent Residence Fee** is refundable if you are not issued a visa or if you withdraw your application. Fees must be paid by bankers' draft. Personal cheques are not acceptable.

SURVIVING THE INTERVIEW

An interview is not always required, but is at the discretion of your visa officer. Do not be alarmed if you are called to interview, it is not necessarily a sign that your application is in jeopardy. Quite the opposite, as the Immigration Division is very busy and not likely to waste time interviewing applicants who do not have a reasonable chance of being accepted. Often the interview is to determine the points to be awarded under the category of Adaptability.

If you are married your spouse will be requested to attend, along with any children over 18.

Being assessed

What can you expect at the interview? As mentioned, your personal suitability will be assessed, as well as your professional qualifications. You can expect the visa officer to ask questions about your current job, past experience and education. Certainly he will want to know why you wish to migrate to Canada and what you have planned once you get there. You want to demonstrate a mature approach. Mention anything that shows you have thought the move through thoroughly and made contingency plans.

Taking the opportunity to prove yourself

The visa officer wants to know that you will be an asset to Canada and that you will adapt well to life there. He will be looking for initiative, adaptability and resourcefulness. What he does not want to see is any evidence that you will not fit in or that you could become a drain on Canadian resources. This applies to all members of your family because, even if they are not accompanying you at this time, they may well do so in the future.

Don't be intimidated by the interview, which is held in a relaxed and informal manner. It is also your opportunity to ask questions, so be prepared if there is anything you want to know. In fact, asking a few questions is another way of demonstrating that mature and thoughtful approach the visa officer is looking for.

COPING WITH OBSTACLES

Hopefully, the process of obtaining the visa will be smooth, but if you run into problems or think your application may not be straightforward you might consider enlisting the aid of an immigration consultant or immigration attorney. These provide similar services, but you need to be aware of the differences, then decide which suits you best.

Immigration attorneys

These are experts in the area of immigration law. They are governed by a professional watchdog body and provide a service for those who are having difficulties with their application, particularly applicants with past convictions or those who do not score enough points under the occupations category.

One of the key differences between an immigration attorney and a consultant is that only attorneys are allowed to attend immigration interviews. In a problematical case this could be very helpful and indeed comforting to the applicant.

What will an immigration attorney do for you?

Although firms vary, basically you are paying the attorney to provide legal advice and assistance in all matters pertaining to your immigration application. Most will:

♦ advise you on the best route to take for your application; for example, an applicant who is refused as a skilled worker may have stood a better chance under the Business Classification

♦ prepare your application forms and all supporting documentation

♦ train you for your interview

♦ attend your immigration interview, providing you with legal representation.

A major firm of immigration attorneys, Brownstein, Brownstein and Associates, warns that 'all too often the skills of an attorney are not called upon until an immigration application has been refused. It is always more difficult to reverse a negative decision than it would have been to provide the best case possible with an attorney from the outset.'

If you feel you are likely to run into problems with your application, that could be advice worth noting.

Paying fees

The scale of fees will differ from firm to firm, so ask for details when you make contact. The address section gives a partial list of immigration attorneys.

Immigration consultants

These firms will help you with the immigration process but differ from attorneys in that they cannot attend the immigration interview and are obviously not as well placed to offer legal advice. However, they do often include settlement advice and business services. Several also assist with job placement. Enlisting the services of a consultant will make things easier for you.

In April 2004, the Canadian Society of Immigration Consultants (CSIC) was set up to serve as a self-regulating body for Canadian immigration consultants. Now, only immigration and citizenship consultants who are members in good standing of CSIC and lawyers who are members of a Canadian provincial or territorial law society will be recognised by the Canadian government. All members are required to keep up with the current immigration rules and regulations by taking refresher and professional development courses.

Paying fees

Balanced against that must be the cost which, again, varies from consultant to consultant. Generally, the more services they provide the larger the fee. See the address section for some immigration consultants.

The choice is yours

If, after carrying out your self-assessment, you think your application will be pretty straightforward you may well choose to tackle the procedure alone. Or you might like to get a second opinion on that all important point score. You can take a free on-line assessment at www.canreach.com In either case, if it doesn't look like plain sailing it could be worth your while to pay an attorney or a consultant.

Do not be overwhelmed by all the rigmarole. In most cases it should be pretty straightforward. And the good news is that, on average, 90 per cent of all skilled worker applicants successfully obtain their visas. So it can't be all that bad!

CASE STUDY

George runs into a problem

Although his points worked out at 73, more than enough to qualify, George encounters what could be a major difficulty with his application. Thirteen years ago, when he was 25, he foolishly drank too much at a party and was convicted of driving while under the influence of alcohol. He paid a fine and has not offended since but this appears on his police record. He contacts an immigration attorney.

'Will that old offence seriously jeopardise my application?'

'I'm afraid it will,' the attorney replies. 'You need to apply for rehabilitation. It was a minor offence and quite some time ago, so we may be able to swing it.'

George hires the attorney, who undertakes the necessary legal work to have George 'rehabilitated'. He is successful in this (although the entire process takes almost two years) and George is eventually granted Permanent Resident Status.

George's occupation of Electronic Engineer appears on the National Occupations Classification List.

		Points
◆	Education (HNC Electronic Engineering)	22
◆	Language (English only)	16
◆	Work experience (16 years)	21
◆	Age (38)	10
◆	Arranged employment	0
◆	Adaptability (wife has BA)	4
◆	George's self-assessed total	73

QUESTIONS ABOUT IMMIGRATION

1. *What is meant by the term 'skilled worker'?*

   This refers to a person with special occupational skills and experience which are transferable to the Canadian labour market. Refer to the National Occupations Classification List to see the occupations that are acceptable.

2. *Will my professional/occupation qualifications be accepted in Canada?*

   Some will, some will not. Sometimes it is just a case of passing an examination or adding an additional qualification. It is up to you to find out if your qualifications relate to the Canadian labour market. You should contact a suitable professional body in Canada. Their names and addresses can be found in *The Canadian Almanac and Directory*. The Canadian Information Centre for International Credentials can also give information on this.

3. *One of my children is remaining in the UK. Does she still need to be included in my application?*

   Yes, if she is less than 19 years of age and unmarried at the time of your application.

4. *I have an aunt living in Canada. Will that help my application?*

   Yes, in that it will increase the number of points you are awarded. Remember that your relative must be over 19 and a permanent resident or citizen of Canada.

5. *I have heard that the procedure is different if I want to go to Quebec.*

   That's right, although it still follows the points system. You do not apply directly to the Canadian High Commission, but to your nearest Quebec Immigration Services office.

6. *Should I hire an immigration consultant or attorney? Will they help me to get my application approved?*

   That is entirely up to you. It is no guarantee of approval, but those who anticipate some difficulties might like to consider this option.

7. *Will I need to attend an interview?*

   That is at the discretion of your visa officer. If you are requested to attend, your spouse and dependent children aged 18 or over will be asked to accompany you.

8. *How long will it take for me to get my visa?*

   This is dependent on a number of factors, but the best way to ensure you get your visa quickly is to be certain you have enclosed all the relevant documents and information with your application.

9. *Will the Canadian Immigration Department help me to find a job?*

   No. That is your responsibility. There are settlement services available, however, and you can find out about these from

Canada Immigration Centres, Canada Human Resources Development Centres and placement professionals.

10. *Once I have Permanent Residence status, how long does it last?*

You must proceed to Canada within one year of issue of the visa. Once there you will remain a permanent resident until you become a Canadian citizen or if you have frequent and/or lengthy absences from Canada.

11. *As a permanent resident, what exactly is my status in Canada?*

You and your dependants have the right to live, study and work in Canada.

You and your dependants are entitled to most social benefits. However, you cannot vote in certain elections and may not be eligible for some jobs that require high-level security clearances.

You are liable for Canadian federal and provincial taxes.

You or your dependants could be deported from Canada if you or they commit serious crimes.

CHECKLIST

◆ Decide which immigration category applies to you.

◆ Study the points system. You need a minimum of 67 to be successful.

◆ Chances are you will need an approved, pre-arranged job in Canada to get a temporary permit.

◆ Students looking for temporary work should contact BUNAC.

◆ It may be worth your while to enlist the services of an

immigration attorney or immigration consultant. Consider this before making your application.

POINTS TO CONSIDER

1. You will need at least 67 points to get a visa as a skilled worker. Use the worksheet in Figure 9 to calculate your points. Do you have enough? If not, how could you increase your total?

2. Are your professional qualifications acceptable in the Canadian workplace? What will you need to do to 'translate' them?

3. Would it be worth your while to hire an immigration consultant or attorney, or do you think you can get your application through without help?

4. The immigration interview is designed to assess your suitability for Canada. They will be looking for initiative, motivation and adaptability. What sort of questions do you think they might ask? And what sort of answers should you give? Is there anything you would like to ask the visa officer?

AM I ELIGIBLE TO APPLY FOR PERMANENT RESIDENCE IN CANADA?		
Factor	**Possible maximum**	**Your score**
Education	25	
Language • First language • Second Language	 16 8	
Work experience	21	
Age	10	
Arranged employment	10	
Adaptability	10	
TOTAL	**100**	

Fig. 9. Immigration eligibility worksheet.

Choosing Location: Where to Work

STUDYING THE GEOGRAPHY

Canada is a vast country, and there are enormous differences of climate, opportunity and lifestyle between the various areas. You may not be able to choose the location of your new job – you may already have an offer lined up, you may be being transferred by your firm or you may simply have already decided on the area that suits you best.

If not, it is worth taking time to look at what is available across the country. There are obvious factors to consider – if you are an avid skier you will not want to be knee-deep in grain fields in the heart of the Prairie Provinces! On the other hand, if you are an electronic engineer aiming to keep at the forefront of your technology, you need to head for an area of fairly intense industry such as Ontario.

The best way to get an overview of locale is to look at each of the ten provinces and two territories separately. The list that follows heads from east to west, and then up a bit to the Northwest Territories and the Yukon.

Newfoundland and Labrador

◆ 405,720 square km

◆ population: 517,000

◆ capital: St John's

- other major population centres: Grand Falls and Windsor

- major industries: include fishing, mining, production of newsprint, oil and gas, hydroelectricity and tourism.

A maritime province consisting of two distinct geographical entities: Newfoundland and Labrador. The climate in Newfoundland is moderate and maritime, with winters that are surprisingly mild by Canadian standards. Labrador has cold winters and brief summers.

New Brunswick

- 73,500 square km

- population: 751,000

- capital: Fredericton

- other major population centres: Moncton and Saint John

- major industries include: food and beverage manufacture, pulp and paper, sawmills, manufacture of furniture and other wood-based industries, metal processing, transportation equipment, processing of non-metallic ores and primary metals, tourism, fishing and agriculture.

A maritime province with a moderate and maritime climate.

Nova Scotia

- 55,491 square km

- population: 937,000

- capital: Halifax

◆ other major population centres: Sydney and Yarmouth

◆ major industries include: fishing and related industries, various manufactured goods, forestry, mining, offshore oil and gas production, tourism, agriculture.

A maritime province with a continental climate (defined as having vivid seasonal contrasts in which long, cold winters are balanced by mild to hot summers) somewhat moderated by the ocean.

Prince Edward Island

◆ 5,660 square km

◆ population: 138,000

◆ capital: Charlottetown, which is the only urban centre (62 per cent of the population live in rural districts)

◆ major industries: include agriculture, tourism and fishing.

A maritime province with a temperate climate.

Quebec

◆ 1,450,680 square km

◆ population: 7,543,000

◆ capital: Quebec City

◆ largest city: Montreal

◆ boasts a highly industrialised and diversified economy with well-developed agriculture, manufacturing and service sectors. Montreal in particular is strong in space and aeronautics, telecommunications, energy and transportation.

An inland province almost entirely surrounded by water (Hudson Strait to the North, the St Lawrence River and Gulf to the south, James Bay and Hudson Bay to the west). Rather varied climate tending to very warm summers in the south and cold winters in both south and north.

Ontario

◆ 1,068,580 square km

◆ population: 12,393,000

◆ capital: Toronto

◆ other major population centres include: Ottawa (federal capital), Thunder Bay, Kitchener, Hamilton, London, Sudbury

◆ major industries: a long list including automobile manufacture, diverse manufacturing, mining, forestry, finance.

It is worth noting that almost 80 per cent of Ontarians live in the southern half of the province, with most of the population in towns and cities near the US border. Ontario is Canada's most productive province, generating approximately 40 per cent of the country's gross domestic product.

Toronto is vying with Vancouver for the title 'Hollywood of the North', as many movies (such as *Chicago*) and television shows are filmed there. In fact, it is reported that the film and television production industry directly contributed $1.16 billion to Toronto's economy in 2002.

An inland province bordering Hudson Bay in the north, with the Great Lakes and St Lawrence River in the south. An extremely varied climate, relatively temperate in the south and more severe east of the Great Lakes.

Manitoba

◆ 650,000 square km

◆ population: 1,170,000

◆ capital: Winnipeg, where 60 per cent of the population live

◆ second largest city: Brandon

◆ major industries: initially based on agriculture, but manufacturing and transportation have increased greatly in importance in recent years; mining.

The first of the three prairie provinces as you travel west, Manitoba is one of the sunniest provinces in Canada. It has a continental climate with great temperature extremes (in Winnipeg, for example, the mean January temperature is -20°C, whilst the July average is about 19°C).

Saskatchewan

◆ 651,900 square km

◆ population: 996,000

◆ capital: Regina

◆ other main city: Saskatoon; together they are home to about one-third of the population

◆ main industry: agriculture; Saskatchewan supplies 28 per cent of Canada's grain production

- other industries: include forestry and mining; research and development is a growing business with an emphasis on agriculture, space technology and biotechnology.

A prairie province, surrounded by land on all sides. Although winters can be harsh the whole province enjoys a hot, dry summer.

Alberta

- 661,185 square km

- population: 3,202,000

- capital: Edmonton

- other main city: Calgary; more than half of Albertans live in these two cities

- major industries: one of the world's most productive agricultural economies, producing approximately 20 per cent of Canada's annual output; livestock production, mining, oil, gas production, forestry, food and beverage processing, production of petrochemicals and plastics, forest products, metals and machinery. The service sector is vital to Alberta's economy, accounting for over 50 per cent of the province's gross domestic product.

Two-thirds of all people in Alberta are under the age of 40, giving the province one of the youngest populations in the industrialised world.

The most westerly of the prairie provinces, with a continental climate. Seasonal contrasts are vivid and extreme resulting in long, cold winters and mild to hot summers.

British Columbia

◆ 947,800 square km

◆ population 4,196,000

◆ capital: Victoria

◆ largest city: Vancouver; 60 per cent of the province's population live in these two cities

◆ major industries: BC's economy is based on the province's abundant natural resources; forestry plays a major role. Next most important economic sector: tourism, followed by mining of metals, minerals, coal, petroleum and natural gas. Agriculture and fishing are important areas. Manufacturing is still largely resource-based but is diversifying into telecommunications and the aerospace and sub-sea industries.

As mentioned earlier, Vancouver vies with Toronto for the title of 'Hollywood of the North'. There are many who would claim she is winning the race, with over 50 movies (*The Fantastic Four, X-Men II* and *Blade Trinity* to name a few) and 20 television series (for example, *The X-Files* and *Smallville*) shot in and around the city since 1998. Vancouver has become the third largest film production centre in the world.

Canada's west coast province. The climate is extremely varied, as is its topography. The coastal region is temperate with lots of rain and some snow; the interior has a continental climate. Other parts of the province could almost be described as desert-like, with extremely hot summers and equally cold winters.

The Northwest Territories

◆ 3,426,320 square km

◆ population: 43,000

◆ capital: Yellowknife, with the largest population at 15,000

◆ major industry: mining (valued at over $800 million)

◆ other industries: oil and gas exploration and development, tourism (the variety of landscapes offer superb fishing, wildlife observation and other outdoor activities).

Canada's most northerly territory, the Northwest Territories stretches from the 60th Parallel all the way to the North Pole. There are two major climate zones: sub-Arctic and Arctic. Whereas the NWT enjoys between 20 and 24 hours of daylight in June it experiences up to 24 hours of darkness in December.

Yukon

◆ 483,450 square km

◆ population: 31,000

◆ capital: Whitehorse, where almost 60 per cent of the population live, the rest spread out in small communities throughout the territory

◆ major industries: a small fishing industry in Dawson City; mining (more than 30 per cent of the economy); tourism plays a fairly large part; about 3 per cent of the population, mainly Aboriginal (who comprise 23 per cent of the population), rely on the fur trade; agriculture is a small but growing industry.

The Yukon occupies Canada's northern west coast and has a sub-Arctic climate. Much of the territory is at high altitude and consequently enjoys relatively warm summers. Winter temperatures average between 4 and $-50°C$ in the south and colder still further north.

Nunavut

Since this book was first written, a new territory, called Nunavut, has been added to Canada's ten provinces and two territories. Spanning 1.9 million square kilometres across Canada's central and eastern Arctic, it is a unique land. Although the territory is large, its population is not, with only approximately 29,000 inhabitants.

Nunavut means 'our land' in Inuktitut, which is the language of the native Inuits who comprise 85% of the population. Theirs is a harsh way of life in the cold, dry Arctic climate. Many still live off the land by hunting or fishing, as did their ancestors for more than 4,000 years.

The creation of the territory Nunavut in April 1999 was a significant achievement – the result of more than two decades of work to produce the most comprehensive land settlement between a state and an aboriginal group anywhere in the world.

It is highly unlikely that anyone from Europe would wish to immigrate to this fascinating but frozen land. Although mining does provide 500 jobs in Nunavut (85% of those employed in mining are non-residents), it is not a way of life many but the hardy and resourceful Inuits themselves could survive.

TEMPERATURE AND PRECIPITATION AVERAGES BY REGION

		January	July	Yearly
Vancouver (British Columbia)				
Temperature	Maximum	5.7	21.7	13.5
	Minimum	0.1	12.7	6.1
Precipitation	Rainfall (mm)	131.6	36.1	1117.2
	Snowfall (cm)	20.6	0.0	54.9
Regina (Saskatchewan)				
Temperature	Maximum	-11.0	26.3	8.9
	Minimum	-22.1	11.9	-3.8
Precipitation	Rainfall (mm)	0.5	58.9	280.5
	Snowfall (cm)	19.2	0.0	107.4
Toronto (Ontario)				
Temperature	Maximum	-2.5	26.8	12.3
	Minimum	-11.1	14.2	1.9
Precipitation	Rainfall (mm)	18.5	76.6	664.7
	Snowfall (cm)	32.3	0.0	124.2
Montreal (Quebec)				
Temperature	Maximum	-5.8	26.2	10.9
	Minimum	-14.9	15.4	1.2
Precipitation	Rainfall (mm)	20.8	85.6	736.3
	Snowfall (cm)	47.7	0.0	214.2
Halifax (Nova Scotia)				
Temperature	Maximum	-0.3	21.8	10.6
	Minimum	-8.9	13.1	2.3
Precipitation	Rainfall (mm)	81.5	97.8	1178.1
	Snowfall (cm)	48.9	0.0	192.6
St John's (Newfoundland)				
Temperature	Maximum	-0.7	20.2	8.6
	Minimum	-7.9	10.5	0.8
Precipitation	Rainfall (mm)	69.3	77.9	1163.1
	Snowfall (cm)	83.0	0.0	322.1

(nb – all temperatures are shown in °C)

Fig. 10. Temperature and precipitation by region.

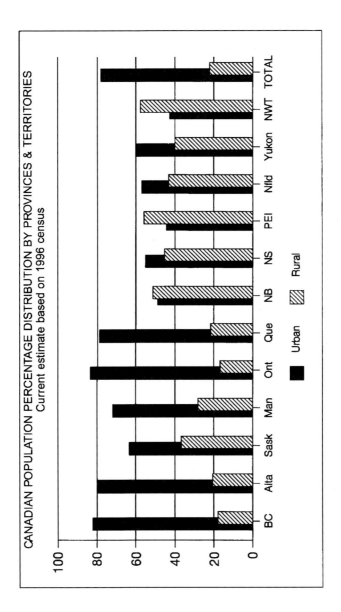

Fig. 11. Population distribution by province.

Getting an overview

To complete your overview of the various provinces and territories, the chart in Figure 10 will give you a good idea of the temperature and precipitation variations across the country.

LOOKING AT DIFFERENT LIFESTYLES

Although bare facts about climate, population and industry can give you a good idea of what the different areas are like, it is often the lifestyle you are really looking at. Let's look at the different regions again, but this time divide them into the seven generally accepted geographical regions, again working westward and then up to the north.

The Atlantic Provinces: Appalachian Region

Referred to as The Maritime Provinces, New Brunswick, Nova Scotia, Prince Edward Island and Newfoundland are the smallest Canadian provinces and are all located on the east coast. Here the lifestyle is unhurried and uncluttered, the scenery magnificent and house prices low.

That said, the opportunities are limited for anyone in a high-tech profession. The fishing industry which once thrived is under serious threat from dwindling fish supplies.

The Great Lakes: St Lawrence Lowlands

The major area to head for if your interests are industry and high-tech. Canada's capital, Ottawa, is located here, so it is the place for anyone wishing to work in government. Also in this region is Canada's largest city, Toronto, which is the home of the world's fourth largest capital market; Toronto's stock exchange is the second largest in North America by volume and third largest by value traded.

The lifestyle in the large cities is intense and bustling, although there is ample opportunity for leisure pursuits, with excellent sporting facilities and fine centres for arts. Housing in Toronto is difficult to find and expensive.

This area contains the majority of Canada's Francophone population and it would be foolish to attempt to settle in Quebec without an excellent command of French.

The Canadian Shield
This area wraps around Hudson Bay and stretches east to Labrador, south to Kingston and northwest as far as the Arctic Ocean. Apart from the region of Kingston in the south, this is a low-tech area with a harsh climate and difficult conditions. The Shield has only a thin layer of soil and is definitely not the place for anyone keen on agriculture.

The Prairies
'The grain bin of the world.' This is an apt description as the Prairies mainly comprise endless fields of wheat and canola. But not only wheat is produced in the Prairies: Alberta is Canada's leading producer of petroleum, and much of the region contains deposits of oil, natural gas and potash. Technology and telecommunications are becoming increasingly important in the large cities. The winters can be bitter and the area is very far inland. Not for you if you have visions of sailing and surfing.

The Cordillera
Where you will find the magnificent Rocky Mountains. Tourism is a major industry in these areas which include the world-famous ski resort, Banff. Not for you if you can't take the cold.

The Pacific Coast

Sometimes known as Lotus Land, this is the destination of more immigrants to Canada than any other area. The temperature is the most moderate of all Canada's regions. People flock from all over the world to enjoy the many activities available on the west coast, from sailing on the Pacific to skiing in the Coast Mountains. The attitude to life here is pretty laid back – it is also called by some the California of the North.

Employment opportunities in Vancouver are quite good, although technology and industry are not as close to the forefront as in Toronto. A lot of employment opportunities will be opening up in response to the successful bid for the 2010 Olympics. Vancouver is a favourite destination for Chinese and Asian immigrants and the exodus from Hong Kong has vastly increased Vancouver's Asian population. Here you will find the famous Chinatown, second in size only to that of San Francisco. Due to the large influx of immigrants and the desirability of the area house prices are very high, particularly in Vancouver.

CASE STUDY

Samantha does some research

Sam's mum is still concerned about her daughter taking off to Vancouver.

'Will you be able to find work there? Do they have a hospital?'

Having visited Vancouver already, Samantha is convinced it is the place for her and is amused by her mother's attitude, as she knows Vancouver is a large cosmopolitan city with several hospitals, nursing homes and clinics.

'Mum, look at this information from the BC Tourist Board. See what a big place Vancouver is and how many hospitals and clinics there are just in the metropolitan area? There are several teaching hospitals, too. I'd like to work in one of them.'

Sam did some further investigation into the area she plans to move to, mainly to set her mother's mind at rest, but in so doing found out more about it for herself.

The Arctic
This area is still largely populated by the Inuit (formerly known as Eskimos) and anyone thinking to move here would have to be made of similarly strong stuff. Although stunningly beautiful, the land is harsh with long, dark and bitterly cold winters. Tourism is a growth industry in this area.

INVESTIGATING OPTIONS
Maybe you have already visited a part of Canada and decided that is where you would like to settle. It's a good idea to make sure that you will be able to get the sort of job you want there.

The various provincial tourist boards have a wealth of information about climate, geography and leisure activities and all are happy to send you a bumper pack of glossy brochures on request. Some have UK bases (see address section). As well as leisure-time information, many packs also contain valuable data about the industries in their areas.

Additionally, there is a wealth of material available on the Internet. The Canadian government's information website at http://atlas.gc.ca has information about things you probably didn't even know you needed to know, as well as useful links. Two other excellent websites showing different lifestyles in different parts of Canada are www.etourist.ca and www.movingto.com, which offers consumer guides for various locations in Canada.

Looking at work opportunities

As Canada's climate and lifestyle varies from area to area, so do the employment opportunities. With a national unemployment rate at one of the lowest points for almost 30 years, there is a good deal of opportunity. Figure 12 shows the average hourly wage in each province. From this you will see the growth pattern from 2004–2005.

It's worth taking a look at how the various professions are faring. The following table gives an idea of trends:

Job losses/gains by profession

Business and personal services	+ 61,000
Agriculture	+ 13,000
Trade	− 32,000
Health and social services	− 22,000
Finance, insurance and real estate	− 21,000

Of course, as everywhere, the employment situation is constantly changing. Keep your eye on current trends by reading publications such as *Canada News*. The Internet is a good source of up-to-date figures. More and more information is being added daily. Each provincial government now has a website providing comprehensive details about their respective areas. See the website section of Useful Addresses.

Finding work through newspapers

There are two national newspapers in Canada. They are *The National Post* (www.nationalpost.com) and *The Globe and Mail* (www.theglobeandmail.com). Both have on-line versions and include job advertisements.Additionally, each of the major cities produces one or more papers which cater for that city and the surrounding area. Most will send you a recent copy on request (send an International Reply Coupon to cover postage), or you can check out their on-line versions to get a good idea of what the job situation is like in the area. See Useful Addresses for details of the daily newspapers published in the major cities.

Looking at wages and employment rates

Average wages vary from province to province. The following shows the statutory hourly minimum wages. Bear in mind that these figures do fluctuate but this will give you an idea of provincial differences.

Province/Territory	Minimum wage (hourly C$)
British Columbia	8.00
Alberta	5.90
Saskatchewan	6.65
Manitoba	7.25
Ontario	7.45
Quebec	7.60
New Brunswick	6.30
Nova Scotia	6.50
Prince Edward Island	6.80
Newfoundland	6.25
Yukon	7.20
Northwest Territories	8.25
Nunavut	6.50

	July 2004	July 2005	% change
British Columbia	18.58	18.85	1.5
Alberta	18.27	19.44	6.4
Saskatchewan	16.69	17.13	2.6
Manitoba	16.66	16.98	1.9
Ontario	19.10	19.81	3.7
Quebec	17.80	18.10	1.7
New Brunswick	14.91	15.26	2.3
Nova Scotia	15.53	16.06	3.4
Prince Edward Island	14.32	14.28	− 0.3
Newfoundland	14.67	15.43	5.2

Fig. 12. Average hourly wages by province (in C$).

ESTABLISHING PRIORITIES

People make the decision to move to Canada for many different reasons. For some it is a question of lifestyle: others seek career opportunities; some are attracted by the wide open spaces. Unless you have already made your choice, or there are overwhelming reasons why only one area is suitable, it might be useful to use the following evaluation list to help you select an area, or a choice of areas – one of the appealing things about Canada is that there is a great deal to choose from.

Ask yourself

1. What is my most important consideration – lifestyle or career?

2. What areas offer the work opportunities I need?

3. What areas offer the leisure activities I want?

4. Am I willing to make any trade-offs between the two?

5. Will the area I have chosen allow me to move forward in my career?

6. Do I mind being limited to one or two main industries or is a variety of opportunity important?

7. Am I looking for a metropolitan lifestyle or does something more isolated and rugged appeal to me?

CONSIDERING THE FAMILY

The above list only looks at your personal preferences and considerations, which is fine if you are setting off on your own. However, if the family is coming along too there are a few other questions to ask.

1. Will there be opportunities for my partner to find satisfying employment, should they so desire?

2. If my partner is not planning to work in Canada are there enough leisure pursuits available? Will it be easy to meet and make new friends?

3. If children are accompanying you, would they be able to adapt to travelling fairly long distances to school or do you need to concentrate on an urban area with schools nearby?

4. Is anybody in the family sensitive to extreme cold? Or extreme heat? Both are facts of life in some areas.

CASE STUDY

George makes a plan

George and his wife realise that they need to know a great deal more about the different areas of Canada before coming to any decision about where to aim for.

'I wouldn't want the girls growing up somewhere where they have no access to culture,' his wife insists.

'But we do want some snow!' the children chime in.

'I think our major priority has to be the work situation,' George says.

George writes to the provincial tourist boards and receives packs of information. He realises that, as an electronic engineer, he will stand the best chance of finding employment in one of the major cities.

'Looks like Vancouver, Montreal or Toronto would be the best places for us to start looking,' he decides.

'Not Montreal,' his wife points out. 'I don't think any of us have good enough French to be happy there, and you'd probably have a problem getting a job.'

The family is learning more about the country and beginning to identify the ideal area(s) for all of them.

CHECKLIST

◆ Canada has many distinctly different areas with enormous variations in climate, geography and lifestyle.

◆ Seventy-six per cent of Canada's population of 32 million live in the major towns and cities.

- In parts of Canada you will need fluent spoken and written French to stand any chance of getting a job.

- The bilingual factor also applies if you wish to work for the federal government.

- Many areas, such as Vancouver, are temperate all year round. Others, like Ottawa and Toronto, experience cold winters and very hot summers. Be aware of these variations.

- Tourist boards are an excellent source of information about the different provinces and territories.

- There are two national newspapers. All the major cities are served by one or more local daily paper.

- Each province has an information website on the Internet.

- The needs and wants of all accompanying family members are important when considering your intended location.

- Trade-offs between desired lifestyle and career opportunities may be needed.

POINTS TO CONSIDER

1. What do you hope to gain from getting a job in Canada? Make a list of the benefits, as you perceive them, of making the move.

2. What are your priorities? Is your career the most important consideration or are you more concerned with general lifestyle?

3. Are you looking for an urban or a rural lifestyle? If the latter, do you have the skills and experience necessary? Would you and your family be able to adapt to a more isolated way of life?

4. Make a list of the areas in Canada where you are most likely to find demand for your skills. Make another list of those areas that most appeal to you from a recreational point of view. How do the two align?

5. Do you have friends or family in Canada? How important is it to live close to them?

6. After investigating the options, make a list of your top three destinations. Will you concentrate your job search in these areas, or are you willing to be flexible?

4

Deciding on the Right Job

GETTING TO KNOW WHAT IS AVAILABLE

Your choice of job in Canada may be obvious. If you are a qualified professional you will probably not be considering changing your career. However, even in this case you need to make sure that your British qualifications translate into Canadian equivalents.

If you are considering different options, there are many places from which you can get information about what is available. Firstly, there are quite a few publications which contain advertisements of positions available in Canada for workers from overseas. These include:

◆ *Overseas Jobs Express*
◆ *Canada Employment Weekly*
◆ *Canada News*
◆ *Jobs Overseas*
◆ *The Expatriate*
◆ *Careers International*
◆ *Graduate Posting*
◆ *Intel Jobs Extract*
◆ *Overseas Employment Newsletter*.

You will find further details of these publications and other job sources in Chapter 5.

The other important factor in your choice of job is immigration requirements, as dealt with in Chapter 2.

Holiday work

If you are looking for a holiday job in Canada you will need to obtain a Work Authorisation Approval Letter. An organisation which specialises in helping students to find temporary work and get an authorisation is:

BUNAC
16 Bowling Green Lane
London EC1R 0QH
Tel: (020) 7251 3472 Fax: (020) 7251 0215
email: enquiries@bunac.org.uk
www.bunac.org/uk

They operate a reciprocal work and travel exchange programme called Work Canada. When you join BUNAC (current cost £5) they send you their *Job Seeker's Guide to Canada* containing all the information you need about finding a job, including applying for a work permit and making travel arrangements.

BUNAC's Work Canada programme is available to young people aged between 18 and 35 and offers a chance to live and work in Canada for three months to a year. It is open to both students and non-students.

To qualify as a student you must be:

♦ a member of BUNAC
♦ a British or Irish passport holder

- aged between 18 and 30
- resident in the UK
- a full-time student on a degree level course or equivalent

or

- a postgraduate level student at a UK college/university

or

- a gap year student with an unconditional offer of a university/ college place.

Current students can spend their summer break in Canada, whilst those completing a final year can stay for up to a year.

Non-students wishing to apply must be:

- a member of BUNAC
- a British passport holder
- aged between 18 and 35
- resident in the UK.

Note that the non-student option can only be used once, whereas students can be part of the programme more than once, provided they are in full-time education between programmes.

The other programme called Gap Canada is for students only and allows for stays of three months right up to a whole gap year. To be eligible you must be:

- aged 18–20
- a British or Irish passport holder

♦ in possession of a guaranteed university place the following year.

You can find out more about these exciting opportunities for young people at BUNAC's website www.bunac.org/uk, where you can also request brochures and download application forms.

Further information about temporary and holiday work can be found in various books, including:

♦ *How to Find Temporary Work Abroad*
♦ *Working Holidays*
♦ *Summer Jobs Abroad*
♦ *Summer Jobs USA* (includes a section on Canada)
♦ *Planning Your Gap Year.*

CASE STUDY

Lucy is overwhelmed

Lucy's application has been approved. She can go to Canada as soon as she completes the spring term. Suddenly, it all seems a bit too real. After all, although she has her aunt to help her find her way, she is heading off for a foreign country with a few hundred pounds in her pocket and no idea of how she will earn her way.

She has a chat with her BUNAC counsellor, who is able to give her an idea of her options and recommends several books about temporary work abroad. After reading these and hearing the experiences of others who have participated in Work Canada she decides she would quite like to move around and see as much as possible during her year out. After all, others seem to have survived and even enjoyed the experience!

Temporary work

Gaining authorisation for temporary work in Canada is a fairly complicated process, although over 90,000 foreign workers achieve it each year. The main thing to bear in mind is that, with very few exceptions, you must have a valid work permit.

First of all you need a job offer from a Canadian employer, which has been confirmed by Human Resources and Skills Development Canada (HRSDC), who must also approve the job being filled by a foreign national. Only at that point can you apply to the Canadian Immigration Commission (CIC) for a temporary work permit.

It is worth noting that there are a few exceptions to this lengthy process. A small number of jobs may be done without a permit. The broad categories are listed below, but you must always check directly with CIC before making any plans or preparations, as inclusion in the list only indicates that the job may be exempt.

Jobs which may be exempt from work permit requirement:

business visitors	foreign representatives
military personnel	on-campus employment
foreign government officers	performing artists
athletes and coaches	news reporters
public speakers	convention organisers
clergy	judges and referees
examiners and evaluators	expert witnesses or investigators
health care students	civil aviation inspectors
accident inspectors	crew members
emergency service providers	

Student work programmes

The Canadian government is keen to make Canada attractive to foreign students. To this end, the *Off-Campus Work Pilot programme* was announced in 2002. This allows foreign students, who are not normally allowed to work without a work permit, to take paid employment for a number of hours per week. If this scheme could work for you, you need to make your application through your post-secondary educational establishment in Canada. You must be registered as a full-time student and have completed at least two consecutive semesters there. Note that successfully obtaining a work permit for off-campus work does not guarantee a job, though. That's still up to you!

By the way, if you are interested in studying in Canada with a view to going on to gain permanent residence, it is worth noting that many provinces encourage this route.

Exchange visits

This is an option for teachers wishing to take up work for a limited period in Canada. Teachers should contact:

The League for the Exchange of Commonwealth Teachers
7 Lion Yard
Tremadoc Road
Clapham
London SW4 7NQ
Tel: 0870 770 2636 Fax: 0870 770 2637
email: info@lect.org.uk

The role of this organisation is to:

- advertise for applicants for exchange

- select suitable candidates through application form and interview

- match the candidates with appropriate qualified overseas teachers

- negotiate exchanges with teachers, schools and employers

- confirm exchanges and provide a detailed service so that good preparatory correspondence takes place about all professional and personal details including accommodation, travel to, from and within, visas, banking, medical care, cultural adjustment

- arrange a pre-exchange briefing conference and orientation conference

- offer full professional, social and pastoral service during exchange

- conduct debriefing and quality control exercises after exchange

- encourage and facilitate longer-term links.

The LECT produces a booklet for UK teachers thinking about exchange to Canada, containing general information and facts. It is available from LECT at the above address.

The Canadian-based association which deals with education exchange visits is:

Society for Educational Visits and Exchanges in Canada
57 Auriga Drive

Nepean, ON K2E 8B2
Tel: (613) 998 3760 Fax: (613) 998 7094
email: info@sevec.ca

Live-in caregivers

The Canadian government now operates a live-in caregiver programme which offers the chance to live and work in Canada temporarily, as well as having the bonus of facilitating permanent immigration should that be your choice.

A live-in caregiver could be providing care in the home for children, the elderly or the disabled. Note that this programme applies only to those giving care in the home. You must meet the following four requirements to qualify for the programme:

1. You have completed the equivalent of a Canadian high school education. Roughly, this would probably mean a range of GCSEs and/or a couple of A levels.

2. You need to have appropriate training and/or experience. This is defined as six months full-time in a classroom setting or 12 months paid full-time employment. The latter must include at least six months' continuous employment in an area related to the job you are looking to do as a caregiver. Put more simply, this could be training or experience in, for example, early childhood education or as a nursery nurse, geriatric care, nursing or first aid. Note that you must have gained this experience during the past three years.

3. You should possess a good level of fluency in English or French.

4. You have a written employment contract which defines your job duties, hours of work, salary and benefits.

The first step in the process requires your prospective employer to submit a request to hire you to the Human Resources Centre Canada (HRCC), who will then confirm the job offer. That's when you can fill in the application forms to gain your authorisation to work as a live-in caregiver.

After you have completed two years in this capacity you can apply for permanent residence whilst still in Canada. As soon as you are notified of a favourable assessment of your application you can apply for an open work permit which allows you to take any job you wish whilst waiting for your application for permanent residence to complete (this can take some time!).

Nurses

It is worth noting that nurses thinking of migrating to Canada, and in particular Alberta, may be able to get help from the Capital Health Authority (CHA). The regional manager of the CHA recently said, 'We are looking for both temporary workers who want to work in Alberta and individuals who want to work in the Canadian healthcare field on a permanent basis'. They offer help to those with nursing and diagnostic imaging backgrounds, assisting with relocations and offers. For further information contact nro@cha.ab.ca (registered nurses) or swingert@cha.ab.ca (diagnostic imaging professionals). You can also visit their website at www.cha.ab.ca

LOOKING AT THE BUSINESS IMMIGRANT OPTION

As discussed in the chapter on immigration, there is another

completely different route to working in Canada: as a self-
employed person or entrepreneur. You will have read in that
chapter what the necessary qualifications are for the Business
Immigration Programme; if you fit the specifications and are
interested in working for yourself there are quite a few factors to
consider.

Attracting the business immigrant

The Business Immigration Programme has proved very successful,
with investors, entrepreneurs and self-employed people accounting
for nearly 8% of all immigrants to Canada. That number
continues to climb. What is the attraction for the businessperson
and entrepreneur?

◆ Canada's wealth of natural resources means that energy is
  cheap.

◆ There is a sophisticated network of transportation systems,
  making goods easily available and facilitating distribution of
  your product.

◆ The workforce is highly educated and provides another
  valuable resource.

◆ Canada has a proactive approach to taxation of Research and
  Development (R&D). Tax treatment of R&D is more
  favourable than in any other industrialised nation, including
  the US. One hundred per cent deduction for current R&D
  expenditure is allowed, as well as for capital expenditure on
  R&D machinery and equipment.

◆ The Government is keen to encourage a successful environment
  for business. The North American Free Trade Agreement

(NAFTA) with the US and Mexico has created a North American trading bloc of 360 million consumers, larger even than the European Union.

♦ The Government has various schemes to encourage participation in the business forum. For example, Small Business loans can provide up to $250,000 for new enterprise.

Investing wisely

For those with investment funds, Canada offers excellent opportunities. Property and business prices are generally half those in the UK. The following will give you some idea of the returns anticipated in business investment areas:

Passive real estate (multi-flat buildings)	10–12 per cent
Semi-active investments (shopping centres, etc.)	10–15 per cent
Active business (hotels, motels, etc.)	15–30 per cent
Active small business (fast-food, retail stores, etc.)	20–40 per cent

Getting advice

The business immigrant option can get rather complicated. Many immigration consultants provide advice and assistance with Immigrant Investor Programmes. You will find a list of these consultants in Useful Addresses.

Choosing the best areas

Report on Business magazine identified the best cities in Canada in which to do business. They were:

♦ Saint John's, New Brunswick
♦ Lethbridge, Alberta
♦ Winnipeg, Manitoba

- Ottawa-Carleton, Ontario
- Missassauga, Ontario.

According to the study these five showed 'the traits that business is currently looking for: dedicated, trainable workforces within short commutes; transportation routes or telecommuncations highways that afford easy access to markets; bottom-line advantages such as low labour and tax costs; infrastructure for telecommunications, pharmaceutical or engineering industries; universities with top research programmes; and pro-business attitude'.

Finding more help
Several organisations offer help and information for Business Immigrants.

The Federal Business Development Bank
This is a government agency formed to help promote and assist small business development and establishment.

> Business Development Bank of Canada
> BDC Building
> 5 Place Ville Marie, Suite 400
> Montreal, PQ, H3B 5E7
> Tel: (877) 232 2269
> email: info@bdc.ca

They have an excellent website at www.bdc.ca which is full of information about starting a business, acquisitions, financing and much more. Well worth a visit.

The Department of Canadian Heritage

They produce a directory of Canadian ethnocultural organisations which are specifically oriented toward business. The directory, called *Multiculturalism Means Business*, can be obtained by phoning 1-819-997 0797. They also have an informative website at www.canadianheritage.gc.ca

Economic Development Departments

The individual provinces offer an invaluable information service for business migrants in the form of brochures, seminars and counselling services. You need to contact the Economic Development Department of the province in which you are interested. Their addresses are in Useful Addresses.

Being self-employed

If you do not intend to set up a business in Canada employing other Canadians, you still may be able to enter as a 'self-employed person'; the requisites for this category are detailed in Chapter 2. The official definition refers to someone who has the ability to purchase a business in Canada that will create employment for themself and make a significant contribution to the economy, cultural or artistic life of Canada. It includes farmers, artists, salespeople and those who can provide a specialised trade or service. Worth investigating if you prefer to go your own way. Self-employed immigrants account for approximately 12 per cent of successful business immigrants each year.

ASSESSING YOUR CHANCES

If you have a British qualification in any profession you will need to find out how it translates into the Canadian market. Some qualifications will be acceptable as they stand, others will need to be augmented by further training in Canada or some sort of examination on arrival. Occupations currently requiring assessment by professional bodies or organisations include:

accountants	occupational therapists
engineers	pharmacists
speech language pathologists	technicians
audiologists	technologists

Checking your credentials

If you feel this might apply to you, get in touch as soon as possible with The Canadian Information Centre for International Credentials (CICIC). This is a very helpful organisation which assists individuals who want to know how to get their qualifications recognised in Canada. They do this by directing you to the appropriate regulatory body or professional association. Note that in Canada the assessment of foreign credentials and qualifications is done by professional regulatory bodies in each province. CICIC has a database of professional associations and provides information on the steps you will need to take to obtain recognition. For those with access to the Internet, the CICIC now has an informative website at www.cicic.ca/, which includes up-to-date information on credential evaluation services. The fact sheets on this site are very helpful. In particular, take a look at www.cicic.ca/factsheets/factsheet2en, which looks at the assessment and recognition of credentials for the specific purpose of employment in Canada and www.cicic.ca/professions/professionsen.asp, which relates to specific professions and trades.

Getting help with your check

There are credential evaluation services which provide an assessment of qualifications for general employment purposes.

They will supply you with a letter of opinion regarding the value of your credentials. If you are a member of a professional body they will probably be able to advise you about the status of your qualifications in Canada. A fee is normally charged. You will find most have information and applications forms available on-line. These services are offered by:

Comparative Education Service, 315 Bloor St W, Toronto, ON M55 1A3. Tel: (416) 978 2185. Fax: (416) 978 7022. Website: www.adm.utoronto.ca/ces

Academic Credentials Evaluation Service, York University, 150 Atkinson Building, 4700 Keele St, North York, ON M3J 1P3. Tel: (416) 736 5787. Website: www.yorku.ca

International Credential Assessment Service of Canada, Inc., 147 Wyndham Street North, Suite 409, Guelph ON N1H 4E9. Tel: (519) 763 7282. Fax: (519) 763 6964. email: info@icascanada.ca

International Credential 3700 Willingdon Avenue, Burnaby, BC, V5G 3H2. Tel: (604) 432 8800. Fax: (604) 435 7033. email: icesinfo@bcit.ca

International Qualifications Assessment Service, Main Floor, 10808-99th Ave, Edmonton, AL T5J 3S8. Tel: (403) 427 2655. Fax: (403) 422 9734. email: IQAS@lab.gov.ab.ca

For the Province of Quebec only:
Service des Equivalences, Ministère des Relations avec les Citoyens et de l'Immigration, 360 rue McGill, Montreal, Quebec

H2Y 2EP. Tel: (514) 873 5647. Fax: (514) 873 8701. See website: www.immigration-quebec.gouv.qc.ca/francais/education/evaluation

CASE STUDIES

Samantha plans ahead

Samantha knows she wants to continue her career as a dietitian once she arrives in Canada, and it is on this basis that she intends to make her immigration application. However, she is concerned that her British qualifications may not be acceptable in Canada.

She writes to The Canadian Centre for International Credentials and discovers that she will have to undertake a short upgrading course. Fortunately, this can be done whilst she is still in Britain.

Samantha completes the course over the next two months on a correspondence basis. She is then given full accreditation when she applies to Canadian Immigration.

George looks at his options

Fully trained as an electronic engineer, George specialised for some years in audio electronics.

'What I'd really like to do is get work in a recording studio, maintaining and upgrading the equipment. I wonder what sort of opportunities are available?'

'Perhaps you could write to some sort of association over there who could give you an idea?' his wife suggests.

George consults the *Canadian Almanac and Directory* (available at larger libraries and on-line at www.mmltd.com.Directories/ Cdn_Almanac.htm) and gets the addresses of the Canadian recording industry associations. From these he finds that he may well be able to find work in that field, particularly in Vancouver or Toronto.

FINDING OUT ABOUT PAY SCALES

The pay structure in Canada is roughly similar to that in Britain in terms of which jobs would be considered poorly paid, medium or well paid. However, salaries tend to be higher on the whole, particularly in the lower paid sections.

You can get an up-to-date and accurate idea of the going rates for various jobs by studying the advertisements and contacting employment agencies. There can be significant differences, depending on locale. Pay tends to be higher in the major cities, such as Vancouver, Montreal and Toronto where accommodation costs are high.

MAKING CHOICES

A great many factors come into your choice of job in Canada. First and foremost will be the basis on which you apply for your visa. Study carefully the Occupations List at the end of this book. After that you need to look at what is available in the area you have chosen and how best you can fill that need. Will you, perhaps, come slightly downscale from your current career status in order to enter an industry that is growing and flourishing in Canada?

The major industries

Here is a brief overview of the major industries, although it is worth remembering that almost any industry you can think of will be represented somewhere in Canada.

- Agriculture. In fact only 7 per cent of land in Canada is arable, but Canada is one of the top exporters of cereal in the world.

- Fishing and fisheries. Canada is the world's leading exporter of fish and seafood.

- Forestry. A massive industry, but potentially troubled due to past over-exploitation of resources and current ecological concerns. Included under this heading is paper and pulp production which continues to flourish.

- Iron and steel. Manufacturing companies spread throughout many parts of Canada.

- Manufacturing. Includes food products, motor vehicles, electrical equipment, chemicals, textiles, aircraft, petroleum products, steel, aircraft and aerospace, industrial and agricultural machinery.

- Mining. Canada's mineral reserves are immense and include zinc, nickel, gold, silver, iron ore, uranium, copper, cobalt and lead.

- Petro-chemicals and gas. Canada is one of the world's foremost petroleum producers.

- Transportation. Understandably, in a country of this size, the transportation industry is very important. Development and manufacture of transportation equipment is a key area.

◆ Tourism. A growth industry, with more and more people from all over the world seeing Canada as an ideal holiday destination.

CHECKLIST

◆ The Immigration Requirements are essential reading.

◆ You might qualify as a Business Immigrant or self-employed person.

◆ The various publications advertising jobs overseas are a good source of employment opportunities.

◆ If you are a student contemplating a year out or short-term employment, contact an organisation specialising in student exchange, such as BUNAC.

◆ If you are a teacher, an exchange visit may be appropriate. Contact The League for Exchange of Commonwealth Teachers.

◆ The Live-in Caregiver programme is an excellent route for those qualified.

◆ You need to find out if your professional qualifications are acceptable in Canada and, if not, what you have to do to make sure they are. Your best contact is the Canadian Information Centre for International Credentials.

◆ Have a look at salary scales, bearing in mind that they vary according to locale.

POINTS TO CONSIDER

1. Will your chosen career get you the required points on the Immigration Selection Criteria? Do you have alternative skills and experience that might gain you more points?

2. Are you interested in short-term work in Canada? The people most likely to succeed in this area are teachers (exchange visits) and students/young people (vacation work).

3. The Live-In Caregiver programme is an excellent route for those with caregiving training and/or experience.

4. What about the entrepreneur/self-employed option? Do you have money to invest in Canadian business? Do you have skills that could make a significant contribution to the economy, cultural or artistic life of Canada?

5. The self-employed alternative can be a bit chancy. Are you willing to take that risk? Do you have sufficient funds to support yourself (and your family) should your business take longer than expected to take off?

6. Are your professional qualifications acceptable in the area of Canada to which you are heading? If not, what will you need to do to bring them into line with local requirements? What can you do to set that process in motion before you leave?

5

Starting the Search Before You Leave

FINDING CONTACTS

To be realistic, unless you are going on a temporary working visit or are being transferred by your current company, you may not get a firm job offer before you leave for Canada. However, it *is* possible and greatly improves your chances with the immigration authorities as well as giving you a much less stressful transition. Where to start?

Using publications

Why not start with the British newspapers? Most carry the occasional advertisement for jobs in Canada. The Sundays are your best bet.

Another possible source of Canadian job advertisements is professional journals, such as *Computer Weekly* or *The Economist*. If there is such a journal relevant to your occupation peruse it regularly.

Specialist publications

There are specialist papers that carry advertisements for overseas jobs. One which concentrates wholly on Canada is:

Canada Employment Weekly
21 New Street
Toronto, ON
M5R 1P7

Tel: (416) 964 6069
Fax: (416) 964 3202
e-mail: info@mediacorp2.com

This is a weekly publication with 32 pages including over 1,000 new job opportunities in 61 major occupation categories. A recent addition is CEW Express, an on-line electronic edition. Visit their website at www.mediacorp2.com for more information and current subscription rates.

A very helpful bulletin available from Canada is:

Overseas Employment Newsletter
PO Box 460
Town of Mount Royal, PQ
H3P 3C7

Anyone interested in working and living in Canada would be well advised to subscribe to *Canada News*. This is an excellent monthly publication packed with current information about lifestyle, immigration and job opportunities. It will also keep you informed of new books and other publications that might help you in your job search. After reading a few issues, you will know more about the Canadian economy and lifestyle than the Canadians themselves. You will also find it a valuable source of advertisements for removal firms, immigration consultants, recruitment firms and more.

Canada News
Outbound Newspapers

1 Commercial Rd
Eastbourne
East Sussex BN21 3XQ
Credit card orders: Tel: (01323) 726040
Email: outboundnews@trbeckett.co.uk

Also try visiting their website www.canadanews.co.uk for all the latest updates on immigration, lifestyle issues, etc.

There are several other sources of advertisements available. The Canadian High Commission has a large selection of Canadian newspapers, magazines and journals and is happy to let you use its reading room. It is advisable to make an appointment.

The City of London Business Library also has a good range of Canadian publications:

City of London Business Library
1 Brewers Hall Garden
London EC2V 5BY
Tel: (020) 7638 8215

A visit to your local reference library can be very productive. There you should be able to find the following three directories which list newspapers, magazines, journals and other publications throughout the world:

Willings Press Guide
Benn's Media Directory
The Ayer Directory of Publications.

The Directory of Jobs and Careers Abroad is useful and can be found at many libraries.

Finally, don't forget the Internet. I have listed a selection of websites later on in this chapter.

Finding out who to contact

There are many books and directories to help you with your search. Two in particular are so comprehensive you might consider getting hold of a copy to keep. They are:

◆ *Canadian Directory of Search Firms 2005 Edition*. The trade reference for Canada's recruitment industry, this directory profiles 2,500 agencies and over 4,000 recruiters in 61 occupation categories. A CD-Rom is included to help you search through all the data in the book.

◆ *Who's Hiring 2005*. Another up-to-date directory, this lists Canada's top employers in 61 categories. It includes human resource, contacts complete with all necessary addresses, telephone and fax numbers and email addresses.

Both these books are printed in Canada and available through *Canada Employment Weekly*.

Two other useful publications available from *Canada Employment Weekly* are:

◆ *The Career Directory 2005*. Contains information on more than 300 degree, diploma and certification programmes to help you match your qualifications with over 1,100 Canadian employers.

♦ *Canada's Top 100 Employers 2005*. As the title suggests, this book profiles employers who lead the way in attracting and retaining quality employees.

You can see more information about all these books (and order on-line if you wish) at www.mediacorp2.com

Publications for temporary work

Several books contain worthwhile information and contacts, including *Living & Working in Canada*, *How to Find Temporary Work Abroad*, *Working Holidays*, *Summer Jobs USA* (includes a section on Canada) and *The Directory of Summer Jobs Abroad*. More information on these and other reference books are in Further Reading.

Using agencies

Contacting employment agencies is possibly the best way of starting your search before you leave for Canada. There are many who deal with overseas placements but not all of them cover Canada. Listed in Useful Addresses are several which do; the list is by no means complete but is a starting point.

As mentioned, you can find out many of the agencies which make placements in Canada by perusing the advertisements in various publications. You can also look in *The Yearbook of Recruitment and Employment Services*, *The CEPEC Recruitment Guide* and *The Executive Grapevine*. The Expat Network produces the *Canada Contact Directory* that gives the names, addresses and phone numbers of hundreds of recruiters. Available from:

Expat Network
2nd Floor, Advertiser House
19 Balflett St, Croydon
Surrey CR2 6TB
Credit card orders by fax: (020) 8760 0469

You can order on-line at www.expatnetwork.com. And while you're there, have a look around this website as, although it is not Canada-specific, there is lots of useful information there.

Your local library is likely to have the following directories which list agencies that make overseas placements:

Directory of Executive Recruitment Consultants
Directory of Assessment and Development Consultants
The Directory of Canada Employment Agencies.

Looking at Yellow Pages

A further source of employment agencies in Canada is the *Canadian Yellow Pages*: most city reference libraries have these for the major cities. However, there may not be a lot of point in contacting local Canadian employment agencies until you have arrived at your destination. The Association of Professional Placement Agencies and Consultants advised me that 'clients normally prefer to hire candidates who are immediately available to commence employment and therefore would be currently settled in Canada'. The spokesperson went on to say that where off-shore technical skills were sought, Canadian agencies would network with their counterparts in other countries. She finished by recommending that new arrivals contact the Association on their arrival, at which time they will redirect you to agencies within your field of expertise.

Using professional placement agencies

The bad news is that there are not many agencies in the UK who can offer much assistance in finding jobs in Canada. Experience has shown that they can tend to be short-lived. Indeed, two that were mentioned in an earlier edition of this book were out of business by the time the book hit the shelves. The good news is that the few that do have Canadian listings often supply contact names and addresses of firms which are not actually advertising. See Useful Addresses for contact addresses.

The news is a bit better with regard to international agencies. These can certainly be contacted before you arrive in Canada and could prove helpful in your search. One such firm is:

RWH International Inc.
620 Wilson Ave
Toronto, ON M3K 1Z3
Tel: (416) 636 3933. Fax: (416) 636 8113
email: info@canadausemployment.com
website at www.canadausemployment.com

Other international agencies are listed in Useful Addresses.

CASE STUDY

Samantha gets a job before she leaves

Sam decides she would like the security of having a job lined up in Canada before she leaves, not least because it would put her mother's mind more at rest!

She decides to invest in the services of a professional placement agency. She locates one that specialises in placing health personnel. For a fee they put her in touch with the Burnaby Outpatient Clinic, which is looking for a consultant dietitian. CV, educational certificates and references are sent. Finally the placement agency arranges for an on-line video interview.

'Good news, Mum. You don't have to worry any more. I've got a job lined up, just outside Vancouver.'

'Will you have to travel far? In all that snow?'

Some mothers will worry about anything, but at least Samantha is set!

Immigration consultants

The popularity of Canada as an immigrant destination and recent changes to the immigration laws and requirements have resulted in a great increase in the number of firms offering immigration advice and assistance. Although the majority of these are reputable there has been concern of late over firms who fail to deliver what they promise. The Canadian government conducted an extensive review of the situation and introduced a regulatory body to monitor consultants.

The decision whether or not to use an immigration consultant is very much a personal one. Many find it is worth paying the fee to have their expert advice and support, others prefer to go it alone.

Have a look at some of the case histories in *Canada News* to learn about people's experiences with consultants, as well as the experience of those who went through the process on their own.

As outlined in Chapter 2, consultants often offer a complete service, including employment assistance as well as immigration advice and counselling. This is probably the best source of professional help with your job search. However, immigration consultants are very unlikely to offer a placement service except as part of their complete package. This means that you would need to pay their fees for immigration counselling and assistance as well.

Be aware also that some consultants operate worldwide and may not have much Canadian input. However, there are many who deal specifically with Canada. See Useful Addresses for a partial list.

Finding temporary work
There is a useful website that lists temporary summer jobs worldwide and sometimes contains Canadian opportunities. Look on the Internet for:

Overseas Summer Jobs at www.summerjobs.com

BUNAC's Work Canada programme is the best option for students looking for gap year placements.

Live-in caregiving is another option for temporary work, as are casual farm labour, work camps and temporary jobs for teachers.

Some contact addresses are listed in Useful Addresses.

Exploring other avenues

At this stage you are trying to spread your net as wide as possible.
Some of the things you try may bear no fruit but, believe me, it is
a fact that the more communications, feelers, applications that you
can get out there, the more opportunities you will get coming
back to you. Often a possibility will appear seemingly out of the
blue and you will wonder why you sent out those dozens of letters
to agencies and employers. But it is the constant outflow of
queries from you that *leads* to that opportunity.

Using contacts

Make use of any and all contacts you can think of. If you have
friends or family in Canada, write or phone them and let them
know that you are on the search. Ask them to send you copies of
their local papers (just the job section will do if postage becomes
expensive) and enquire if they know of any job openings in their
area. Perhaps they could get an application form from their place
of work that you could fill in on spec. If you do something like
that, be sure to mention your connection. Everything helps.

Over the past few years, small relocation 'experts' have begun
springing up. These are usually people who have successfully
navigated the emigration process themselves and offer (for a fee of
course) their advice and support. I suspect that most have real
estate connections also, but they can be very helpful. Here follows
a small selection.

If you don't have any contacts in Canada and are thinking of
moving to Alberta you could contact Helen Willy. She is an estate

agent (or realtor) who emigrated from England to Canada in 1995 and now writes regularly for *Canada News*. She is very happy to provide information to prospective immigrants and will send relevant newspapers and job listings for the cost of postage only. Although she obviously hopes to benefit from helping you there is no obligation at all. Helen can be reached at:

Tel: (403) 995 1858
Fax: (406) 995 1859
email: helenwil@telus.net
or visit www.homeiscanada.com

Also located in Alberta are Ian and Jayne Wisdom who run Canilink Relocation, advising on relocation and settlement. You can contact them for a free brochure at:

48 Chapparal Drive SE
Calgary, AB T2X 3J6
Tel: (403) 254 8051
Fax: (403) 254 8053
email: canilink@shaw.ca

If you're BC-bound, try Sue and Frank Gerryts at:

Tel: (604) 764 3563
email: sue@relocation2BC.com

CASE STUDY

Lucy casts her net wide
Lucy continues to try to find some temporary work before she

leaves. She gets several leads from the Internet but before she can chase these she gets a phone call from her aunt.

'Bob's Burger Bar just down the road from us is going to be taking on extra help come June. That's when their busy season starts. I mentioned you to him – told him you were arriving in May. He's going to hold a place open for you provisionally. It's not much, just waitressing, but it will be something to start you off.'

Lucy is well on her way to a successful working tour of Canada.

Secondment or transfer

Another possibility is secondment or transfer within the company you are currently employed by. This would only apply to a fairly large firm that has offices in Canada, but if this is the case make enquiries of your personnel officer. Beware though, if this approach comes to nought it could jeopardise your career path so only try it if you are committed to the move.

Links Abroad

Canada News operates a club called Links Abroad which is a contact base for anyone thinking of living or working abroad, as well as for those who have friends and relations abroad.

Whilst you may not directly find job opportunities through this association, it's all part of making contacts. And as a plus you will be eligible for lots of discounts all over the world, including special migrant airfares – very useful once you have succeeded in your job search!

More ideas

How else can you spread your net? There is always the option of placing Situation Wanted ads in Canadian newspapers and relevant journals. You can find the appropriate ones through the sources listed above.

Your professional body or trade union may be able to advise you of opportunities in other countries including Canada.

Several Canadian provincial governments have offices in the UK where you can usually find up-to-date listings of vacancies in the provinces served.

Going on-line

A big change in job search technique has come about recently. Don't worry – it's good news. More and more employers and job hunters are using the Internet. A few years ago you could find the occasional information site but often these were out of date or abandoned within months. However, there is now a wealth of information and leads for the job seeker.

Those who are already familiar with the Internet won't need to be told how to find these sources. However, you might find the list of current sites in Useful Addresses helpful in your search. Of course, being on the Internet already does give you the advantage of being able to set up your own website if you wish. To be honest, it is doubtful that prospective employers spend time looking at individual websites. They are far more likely to go to the comprehensive listings. But cast your net (or in this case web) wide. It can only help.

If you have not yet entered this world of global information, don't be put off by unfamiliarity or technospeak. It really is very simple and you don't need your own computer or Internet connection to make use of what is available. Many public libraries now have PCs connected to the web. Minimal charges are made and in some cases it is even free, and there's bound to be a computer-wise librarian to help you get sorted.

The relevant sites fall into two main categories: information and actual job listings. Several sites are listed in the relevant sections in this book and in Useful Addresses, and there are bound to be many more. Here, however, are a few to get you started.

Websites providing useful general information:
Citizenship and Immigration www.cic.gc.ca Contains details regarding visas, immigration quotas, career opportunities and lifestyle. This is probably the most valuable and important site for anyone wishing to work in Canada. The Canadian government seems to have entered the world of electronic communication in a big way and has packed this site full of useful information, as well as all the forms needed for the various types of immigration application.

The Government of Canada's information site www.canada.gc.ca This includes information about jobs and organisations. Features up-to-date news from each province.

Each provincial government has its own website: The addresses are listed in Useful Addresses at the back of the book.

A comprehensive guide to careers, education, training facilities, jobs and immigration around the globe can be found at www.career tips.com

The Canadian Almanac contains just about all the facts, figures and information you could ever want to know about Canada. It can be accessed on-line at www.mmltd.com/Directories/Cdn_Almanac.htm

This is only a small selection to get you going on your web search. Most of these sites, and those listed in Useful Addresses, have links to many more interesting and useful sites. So be prepared for a long and fruitful journey.

Websites with job listings or links

There is a wealth of sites offering job listings throughout the world, although many are not Canada-specific, so you may have to be patient in your search. Be aware that there are fakes as well as real gems, so just use your common sense. In particular, be wary of any site requesting money or financial details. I would recommend starting with the Government of Canada's own site at www.jobbank.gc.ca You might also try:

Canada Jobs   www.canada.plusjobs.com

Note that this site has comprehensive links to province- and city-specific listings.

Plus Jobs   www.plusjobs.ca
Actual Jobs   www.actualjobs.com

Jobs Abroad	www.jobsabroad.com
Escape Artist	www.escapeartist.com/jobs/overseas
Find a Job	www.find-a-job-canada.com/overseas
Job Search in Canada	www.job-search-in-canada.com

There are many more. I suggest you just type 'Jobs Canada' into a good search engine such as Google and you'll be off and running.

The Internet is expanding daily and offers up-to-date information and leads for the job seeker. It is particularly valuable for anyone trying to find a job in another country. No more airmail delay – the local candidate will see a new advertisement no sooner than you, even though you are thousands of miles away.

CASE STUDY

George sets his search in motion

George realises that the chances of getting a definite job offer before he arrives in Canada are slim, but wants to set the search in motion.

'Aren't you spending a lot of money on all these subscriptions?' his wife asks. 'And I shudder to think what our phone bill will be like with the amount of time you're spending on the net.'

'An international job search is bound to take some money,' George replies. 'But it will pay off in the long run. There are a lot of websites to check. And the publications will be useful to me once we arrive in Canada, too. And the sooner I put myself into the job market, the better.'

George is being realistic. An international job search *does* use up resources – both time and money – but he is going about it exactly the right way.

MAKING YOUR INITIAL APPROACH

Replying to job advertisements

Let's look first at replying directly to companies that are advertising for staff. How can you make your application stand out from the crowd?

Most important is a CV (or résumé) that really works. See the next section for some tips. Of almost equal importance is your covering letter. A CV is a fairly dry and blunt statement of your qualifications and experience, but in the covering letter your personality and enthusiasm should be apparent. Bear in mind, however, that a more formal style will probably be appropriate if you are replying to a personnel office in the UK; a lighter toned letter may be better suited if the application is to be mailed directly to a Canadian address.

Writing covering letters

Your covering letter should include information as to whether you have, or have applied for, your Canadian Permanent Resident Status or Employment Authorisation. This information is important for the employer, who needs some idea of when candidates will be available. Give some indication of when you hope to receive your Authorisation if you do not have it already.

What to include

Although the information will be in your CV, direct the prospective employer's attention to any experience or training that is particularly relevant to the position you are applying for. It doesn't do any harm to blow your own trumpet a bit! The great British art of the understatement is not understood or appreciated by most Canadians who tend more to the 'If you've got it, flaunt it' principle.

Employers usually appreciate a brief mention of how you came to know of the vacancy. Often they advertise in several publications and like to get an idea of which ones are working best for them.

References and certificates

References are not necessary at this point, although you will have mentioned in your CV that they are available on request. The same applies to educational certificates. However, you may feel that including these documents will add weight to your application, in which case it is perfectly appropriate to send copies at this point.

Providing contact numbers

Particularly if you are applying to a Canadian address, an email address and fax number can prove very useful. It could be to your advantage if an employer can reach you more quickly than another candidate. It is usually possible to 'rent' a fax address locally if you do not have a machine yourself. Look in *Yellow Pages* under Facsimile Bureaux and Secretarial Services.

More and more of this sort of communication is done via e-mail, so it definitely advantageous to have an e-mail address. Canadian companies and employers make extensive use of this facility.

Checking your covering letter

To sum up, you should try to include all of the following in your covering letter (whilst making it snappy and succinct!):

Emphasise your suitability for the job, pointing out relevant experience and qualifications in your CV.

♦ State why you want this particular job.

♦ Give some idea of your availability.

♦ Include telephone number and fax number and/or e-mail address if possible.

♦ State how you became aware of the vacancy or (in the case of a speculative letter) the company.

♦ Try to include something that gets just a bit of your personality across.

A final note about presentation. If anything this is even more important when applying to a Canadian employer than it is with a British application. Use good quality paper, and a printer that gives a dark and clean impression. If you do not have access to such equipment use a secretarial service. A small job such as cover letter and CV will not cost much.

Contacting agencies

Much of the above applies to contacting agencies as well. One of the major differences is that they are likely to send you a comprehensive application form before going any further. A note on these: they are tedious and filling them in soon becomes a boring, repetitive task. Worse than that, the information asked for is invariably on your CV anyway! Resist the temptation to ignore them or to write 'See CV' across the questions. Most agencies employ someone to input the data from these forms onto their database. That person is not employed to extract the data from your CV and, more importantly, might not put it in the form you want. So bite the bullet and fill in the forms as comprehensively as possible.

Once again, increased Internet use is making changes in this area. Many agencies now provide forms that can be filled in on-line, which makes the process a bit easier.

Do, however, beware of sending your CV and covering letter as e-mail attachments. Unfortunately, the incidence of computer viruses spread through the Internet is also on the increase, and some firms will simply not open attachments. Only send an attachment if invited to do so. If not, include your CV, etc. in the body of the e-mail. Otherwise it may never be seen.

Supplying references

An agency will probably also ask you at this stage for references. Although a name, address and telephone number might be sufficient for a UK-based agency it may not be appropriate for one based in Canada. Ask referees to write a reference for you in advance, addressed To Whom It May Concern. Send photocopies of these to the agencies, along with addresses, fax, e-mail and telephone numbers.

The covering letter

Once again your covering letter is very important. If you are replying to an advertisement for a specific job you can follow the guidelines above, with an additional note about being interested in any other similar vacancies. If, however, you are contacting an agency to register with them and to be considered for any jobs in your field you will want to give a good idea of your experience and what sort of jobs you are qualified for and interested in. You may have skills that apply in several fields: be sure to point this out in your letter.

WRITING ON SPEC

Yet one more way to cast your net wide is to write speculative letters to companies which might need your skills. Most of these cold contacts will elicit no response, but there is always the possibility that your letter and CV will arrive on the personnel officer's desk on the very day that she despaired of ever finding the right person to fill that post which you were obviously born for.

Look for large companies that may require your expertise. If your field is administration your target area will obviously be pretty broad. If your skills are more specialised you will find fewer prospective employers to write to but will probably have a better chance of hooking one.

Using libraries for contacts

If you are able to get to London, a good place to find the names and addresses you want is the City Business Library, the address for which is given earlier in this chapter. They have the *Yellow Pages* for all cities and towns and you will find more addresses than you can ever want.

Any fairly large city library will having listings of Canadian companies. Ask the reference librarian – they are invariably helpful. In particular look out for the *Canadian Key Business Directory*, published by Dun and Bradstreet, which gives a profile of the top Canadian firms and includes names, addresses, telephone numbers, and the names and titles of executives who run each company. It also contains a useful geographical listing. Consult also the *Canada Business Directory*.

Contacting international companies

A good speculative approach is to contact British companies which have branches in Canada, as well as Canadian firms with branches in the UK. This removes the possible obstacle presented by the great distance between you and your prospective employer. This can be one of the best ways to find a job before applying for Employment Authorisation, thus greatly enhancing your chance of getting immigration approval. There is an excellent directory published by Dun and Bradstreet, *Who Owns Whom*, which gives you this information and which you should find in almost any reference library.

Following this tack of contacting international companies, you could try contacting the Chambers of Commerce listed in the address section that may provide you with lists of British companies in Canada and Canadian companies in Britain.

Writing the covering letter

When making speculative enquiries your covering letter is possibly more important than the CV itself. Follow the general rules stated above but emphasise the trumpet-blowing even more. You really are selling yourself, and doing it cold which, as any salesman will attest, is the hardest thing of all. You need to tailor your letter to the type of firm you are writing to as well as to the sort of job for which you are looking.

TURNING A CV INTO A RÉSUMÉ THAT WORKS

Although we have been referring to CVs, the term in use in Canada is Résumé. Although similar to a CV, a résumé differs slightly in both format and content. Figure 13 shows a typical Canadian-style résumé. A CV tends to include more personal details than you will find on a résumé.

Types of résumé

You have a choice of type of résumé. Figure 13 shows the chronological résumé. Figure 14 is an example of the functional résumé, which categorises your experience into areas of skill and expertise. The chronological résumé is the usual form but either will be acceptable and you should choose the one that best highlights your abilities and suitability. You may wish to draw up one of each sort and decide which is most appropriate for each application.

Note that both examples cite a Job Objective. This is not absolutely essential and appears to be an American innovation. However, Canadian employers are becoming increasingly accustomed to seeing this on résumés. This is certainly an area in which you can customise your résumé for optimum results.

'Tweaking'

Which brings us to a very important point: tailoring your résumé to fit the job for which you are applying. If you have access to a word processing programme this need not be an onerous task. It really is worth taking the time to check your résumé each time you send it out, to see if it really shows off the skills required for a specific job. It is largely a question of emphasis. Say, for example, that you are applying for a middle-management position

Résumé of
Jeffrey Gilbert

123 Green Lane
Godmanchester
Cambs PE18 3TR
United Kingdom
Tel: 44-1480-388678
Fax: 44-1480-388542
Email: jg@whatever.net

JOB OBJECTIVE: R&D Manager

EMPLOYMENT

Date:　　　　1997 to the present.

Employer:　　Inx Printing Technologies plc, St Ives, Cambs, UK.
　　　　　　　Design and manufacture of industrial ink jet printers.

Position:　　Research and Development Group Leader.
　　　　　　　Project management, staff placement and supervision,
　　　　　　　budget preparation and finance control for the group.
　　　　　　　Technical involvement in all aspects of the projects. Long-
　　　　　　　term product planning. Other responsibilities include
　　　　　　　patent preparation, quality issues, and deputising for the
　　　　　　　Director.

Date:　　　　1993 to 1997.

Employer:　　Neve Electronics Ltd, Melbourn, Herts, UK.
　　　　　　　Design and manufacture of audio recording consoles.

Position:　　Planning Manager.
　　　　　　　Planning, monitoring and progressing company-wide
　　　　　　　product development programmes. Project planning
　　　　　　　encompassed all stages of product development from
　　　　　　　concept to customer training across all departments.
　　　　　　　Development of long-term planning strategies for R&D,
　　　　　　　manufacturing and sales. Responsibilities included budget
　　　　　　　preparation, staff placement, work scheduling and project
　　　　　　　expenditure.

Date:　　　　1985 to 1993.

Employer:　　DA Jet Ltd, Cambridge, UK.
　　　　　　　Design and manufacture of industrial ink jet printers.

Position:　　Project Manager.
　　　　　　　Preparation and management of both short- and long-
　　　　　　　term product development strategies. Responsible for
　　　　　　　coordination and management of project resources and
　　　　　　　administration of engineering budgets and schedules
　　　　　　　within R&D. Senior design authority, responsible for
　　　　　　　engineering standards and project development
　　　　　　　equipment. Staff supervision and placement (20 plus).

Fig. 13. Chronological résumé.

Date:	1981 to 1985.

Employer:	Roband Electronics Ltd, Crawley, Sussex, UK.
	Industrial and military power supply manufacturer.

Position:	Senior Design Engineer.
	Design of industrial and military power supplies and fail-safe control systems to military standard 05-21. Research and development of switching converters. Prototype development supervision, and production liaison. Environmental testing and field trials supervision.

Date:	1977 to 1981.

Employer	General Post Office (Telecommunications Division), UK.
	Telecommunications.

Position	Technical Trainee.
	Apprenticeship in electrical and electronic engineering. Various work assignments throughout the G.P.O. Block release to Openshaw Technical College.

EDUCATIONAL ATTAINMENT

1978–1981	Openshaw Technical College, Cheshire, UK.
	HNC in Electrical and Electronic Engineering.

1972–1978	Long Road Secondary, Sale, Cheshire, UK.
	General Certificate of Education A-Levels (equivalent to post high school diploma) in Maths, Electronics, Physics and Telecommunications.

ADDITIONAL COURSES

1990	Microprocessor Applications
1991	'C' Programming
1999	Electro-Magnetic Compatibility
2000	Basic Company Finance
2001	Total Quality Management

ADDITIONAL INFORMATION

Member of the Institute of Patentees and Inventors.

With over twenty years' experience in the electronics industry, I have developed a broad knowledge base in both engineering and project management. Because of my knowledge of other disciplines such as mechanics, pneumatics, and fluidics, I can apply my problem-solving abilities to most areas of a project. This is particularly valuable in project management roles.

Fig. 13. continued.

RÉSUMÉ

JOHN CROSS

728 Whitehorse Lane
Brentford
Middx TW8 0NY
United Kingdom
Tel: 44 1208 847 9665
Fax: 44 1208 847 6097
Email: jc@whatever.net

JOB OBJECTIVE:
Senior Sound Engineer or Producer of various forms of popular music, including dance, rock and easy listening.

ENGINEERING EXPERIENCE:
Senior Engineer at Blue Moon Recording Studio, London, UK. Worked on CD albums released by chart-topping GirlzOwn and Mandy White.

Engineer at SuperSound Studio, London, UK. Responsible for pre-mixes.

Apprentice Engineer at Roll 'Em Studios, Lincoln, UK.

PRODUCTION EXPERIENCE:
Producer at Pinewood Studios, Manchester, UK. Produced various artistes including Conqueror and Fave-Rave. Produced and mixed the top twenty CD album 'My Little Unicorn' by the Triplettes.

EDUCATION:
Higher National Diploma (equivalent to post high school diploma) in Sound Recording and Production Services, Sinclair School of Sound, Lincoln, UK.

General Certification of Education O-Levels (equivalent to high school diploma) in Maths, Design and Communication, English, Photography, Science.

OTHER DETAILS:
Member of the Association of Professional Recording Services. Fully computer literate with experience of various graphic and audio software programmes.

Fig. 14. Functional résumé.

with a firm that manufactures and supplies surgical equipment to doctors and hospitals. You do not have experience of this product, but your management skills are exemplary. You would 'tweak' your résumé so that even greater emphasis was given to these assets. You would also mention the voluntary work you did at a blood donor clinic. If the firm supplied food products the latter would be irrelevant, although you would still emphasise the former.

Explaining terms

When listing your qualifications remember that some letters and designations may mean nothing to the Canadian employer. If you are a MICE by all means say so, but write it as Member of the Institute of Civil Engineers. Similarly some educational terms may be unknown. For example, A-Levels do not exist as such in Canada. So list them, but put in brackets 'equivalent to post-high school diploma' or something similar. O-Levels or GCSEs would be 'equivalent to high school diploma'. Most university-level degrees translate well, although different classes of degree should probably be spelled out.

Leave no gaps

Just as you want to draw attention to the high points of your education and career, you do not want your potential employer focusing on the difficult areas. Most of us have something in our career past that looks a bit odd or needs explaining – gaps in employment, for example. Try to limit the negative impact and even, if possible, turn it into something positive.

Explaining employment gaps

Do not leave employment gaps unexplained or try to cover up the fact. If you were looking for a job, say so. If you did any training during that period, be sure to point it out. That illustrates a proactive approach. Or if you took some time out to travel the world, say just that. The recruiter may admire your spirit of adventure! At least he won't be imagining you spending a year as a couch potato.

Explaining education gaps

Gaps in your education can cause a problem too. Perhaps you began a degree course but did not complete it or gain the qualification you were studying for? Should you omit the fact or give details and risk having the prospective employer think you a failure? It is possible to make a plus point of even this. Outline what you did achieve (eg, first year BA Business Studies) and, if possible, any plans you have to complete the course. Whatever you do, don't leave a gap. As with the employment gap, the recruiter will wonder what you were doing for two years and may well come up with something less favourable.

Explaining career changes

Another potential problem area is frequent career changes. There is a fine line between being perceived as a flexible go-getter or as shiftless and unreliable. If you have moved about quite a bit during the course of your career there is no disguising it. Try instead to highlight other areas which might reinforce your reliability and commitment – for example, completing a long degree course or having held positions of responsibility. Do not try to explain the frequent changes by complaining about the companies for which you worked. That just makes you seem a moaner.

Effective presentation

Once again, presentation is all important. You want to make a good job of selling yourself, but not at the risk of the recruiter losing interest. A résumé for someone with ten to 20 years' experience will likely run to two pages. More than that is not advisable. If you really do have a long list of credentials and experience you may need to resort to providing a one-page summary followed by the more detailed version, but in almost every case two pages should suffice. Those with shorter careers to date should try to get it all on one page. What you *don't* want is one-page-and-a-bit! Either squeeze it into one or elaborate to two full(ish) pages.

It is very likely that you will be sending your résumé and letter via e-mail. That is no reason not to make it as visually attractive as possible. Take care with your e-mail message – check spelling and grammar as thoroughly as anywhere else. Send a copy by post as well – international recruitment can be a lengthy business and there is no substitute for a prospective employer holding your well-presented application in their hand.

Even though you are probably going to be sending the résumé and letter by air mail, don't go for lightweight paper. A good, heavy bond gives a subconscious and immediate impression of reliability and solidity. What was said earlier about the cover letter applies even more to the résumé itself. The type must be bold, clean and clear. Photocopies are acceptable as long as they are of good quality. You might even like to jazz the whole thing up by using a coloured paper – nothing too garish, but a very light blue or buff will make your résumé stand out from the rest without shouting.

Your résumé checklist

It is not possible to overstate the value of customising your résumé to fit the job applied for, so not all of the above will apply in each case. You should, however, be sure to include the following on every résumé:

♦ Name, address and telephone number. Fax number and e-mail address if applicable.

♦ Full details of your educational attainment. Be sure to translate your qualifications into terms understood by Canadians, if necessary.

♦ Details of your career to date. Give names of employers and dates, and outline your duties and responsibilities.

♦ Other relevant information such as membership of professional associations, public offices held and other skills. There is excellent scope for 'tweaking' in this area.

IMPRESSING THE CANADIAN EMPLOYER

If you do all the above you will impress any employer! But what we want to look at here is your impact specifically on the Canadian employer. It is true that most Canadians love all things British, so play on that. It is one of your assets. Although you want to avoid the great British understatement, a little bit of British eccentricity might not go amiss. Just a touch, mind! Do not attempt this if you are applying to a Francophone company.

Overcoming competition

You will often be competing with resident Canadians for a position. What can you offer that they cannot? In addition to a bit of 'Britishness' you have one other inherent asset. You are obviously adventurous and not frightened of new challenges, otherwise you would not be attempting to embark on a career in a new country.

The other side of the coin is that a prospective employer could wonder if you are going to stay the course: are you going to get fed up with Canada and wander off? The way around that is to emphasise your intrepid and flexible nature whilst indicating your commitment to your new life in Canada. Canadians are susceptible to flattery regarding their country so you could say something complimentary about Canada and how much you are looking forward to being part of its growth.

Selling yourself

What exactly is the Canadian employer looking for?

- experience
- training and education
- confidence
- enthusiasm.

Additionally, a second language is a great asset. A good command of French is vital if you choose to work in either a Francophone area such as Quebec or in government. Other languages are useful too due to Canada's multicultural nature. If you are thinking of getting a job in Vancouver, for example, Cantonese would help tremendously.

The most important message as far as getting a job in any part of Canada is concerned is *sell yourself*. Let employers know what you can do for them. Highlight your assets and skills. Do something to make yourself stand out from the crowd. Present your experience as favourably as possible. If you are used to living and working in Britain that may not come easily, it isn't the British way. But it *is* the Canadian way and you need to get a handle on it in order to succeed.

CHECKLIST

◆ The British newspapers will occasionally have advertisements for jobs in Canada.

◆ *Canada Employment Weekly* has extensive listings for job opportunities in Canada.

◆ *Overseas Jobs Express* carries ads for jobs world-wide, including some in Canada.

◆ *Canada News* has articles of real interest to those planning to move to Canada.

◆ *The Canada Contact Directory* is a very useful guide to employment agencies which recruit for Canada.

◆ Some British firms have offices in Canada, some Canadian ones have branches in the UK. These are ideal targets for your speculative letters.

◆ Check out *The Canadian Directory of Search Firms* and *Who's Hiring*.

◆ Make use of all your contacts, including friends and family in Canada.

◆ There are a number of sites on the Internet that advertise Canadian postings, as well as those that allow you to try to sell yourself. Because communication is immediate you will not suffer the disadvantage of distance.

POINTS TO CONSIDER

One of the key messages of this chapter was *sell yourself*. That isn't always easy. You need to do it in a way that suits you, to be comfortable with it. If blowing your own trumpet does not come easily to you, try the following:

1. Have a look at your experience, including your education. What are the high points? What do you have that makes you better than the next applicant?

2. Having identified your strengths, think about how you can put them across. If you are someone people feel comfortable talking to, for instance, that will not be apparent from your CV. You will have to make a point of it if it is relevant to the job you are applying for. How can you do that? Have you perhaps been involved in some voluntary work that makes it obvious, or will you have to be bold and just state the fact?

3. Get a friend to help now. Ask him to pretend that he does not know you, then give a one- or two-minute speech that outlines your career and experience. Try to accentuate all your positive assets, but tell the truth about your accomplishments. When you have finished, your friend should tell you what he has learned about you from your précis. Compare that with what you both know about your skills and experience. Then try it again, with even more emphasis on the positive.

Before you can start selling yourself you need to make contacts.

4. Which job sectors are you interested in? Which agencies deal with placements in these fields?

5. Have a look at the advertisements in the overseas jobs papers and on the net. Are any close to your skills and interests? Are they placed by agencies or individual companies? If agencies, you can contact them for similar opportunities. If individual companies, you could write a speculative letter asking if they have any openings in your field.

6. Do you know anyone who lives in Canada, or anyone who knows anyone who lives in Canada? Can you take advantage of this contact?

7. Think about tailoring your CV/résumé for different opportunities. Could you cut the work involved by having one generic résumé and three or four variations?

8. How can you make your résumé and covering letter stand out from the crowd?

9. Most Canadians love all things British. How do you feel about trading on that? Would you be embarrassed?

6

Arriving in Canada

SETTING OUT

You have your visa, you know where you're headed, and you either have a job lined up or a good idea how to go about getting one and enough resources to keep you afloat while you search. Time to set out. The preparations you will need to make depend on your personal circumstances and whether you are heading to Canada for good or for a limited period. In either case there are some essentials to be sorted before you leave.

Banking arrangements

Be sure to inform your UK bank of your move. You may decide to keep the account going for a while, even if you are permanently relocating to Canada. It is a good idea to do this, as UK payments frequently need to be made after you have been away for a few months or more and it is easier to do this from a UK account. On-line banking, readily available now, makes this much easier. If you do decide to close the account make sure you clear any direct debits or make alternative arrangements for paying them.

Make sure you are taking sufficient money to tide you over until you are fully settled in. Travellers cheques are best for ready cash. If large sums of money are involved (say, the proceeds of the sale of your house) it is best to let the UK bank know that you will shortly be requesting transfer of the funds. Once you have started an account in Canada you will advise them of the details and the money will be transferred.

It's a good idea to ask for a letter of introduction from your bank. This will make opening an account in Canada simpler.

Tax and National Insurance
Inform the tax office of your move. There will be adjustments to be made in the form of a rebate or tax owing by you. If you have been self-employed, or had any significant income from sources other than regular employment, it is worth hiring an accountant to sort out your accounts before you leave. If there are any queries it is so much easier to deal with them from the UK.

Similarly you will need to inform the Social Security office of your plans. You should contact:

HMRC
Contributions Agency Overseas Branch Centre for
Non-Residents
Parkview Benton
Newcastle-upon-Tyne NE98 1ZZ
Tel: 08459 154811

Be sure to take any relevant tax and National Insurance documents with you to Canada, including your National Insurance number.

Tidying up hire purchase arrangements
Make sure that these are all up to date and either make final payments or arrangements to continue your payments from Canada. (This is one of the instances when it is simpler to maintain your UK bank account for a while.)

Arranging insurance and pensions

You will need to sort out all your other insurances: life, property, etc. Make sure your goods are adequately insured in transit and on arrival in Canada. Contact your car insurers and get some record of your claims history, otherwise you may well find yourself paying full premiums if you are unable to prove any no claims history.

Contact the administrators of any pensions plans you contribute to and discuss future arrangements.

Firms specialising in finance for emigrés are listed in Useful Addresses.

Redirecting subscriptions and mail

Make sure you have either cancelled or redirected any subscriptions and make arrangements with the Post Office to have your mail redirected. It is advisable to pay to have your mail sent on for at least a year. Even if you think you have informed everybody you know of your new address, it is easy to miss somebody. You wouldn't want the letter from long-lost Great Aunt Gertrude's solicitor informing you that you have inherited her fortune to be returned Address Unknown!

Utilities

If you are making a long-term or permanent move be sure that your gas, electricity and phone bills are paid up. If your move is short-term make suitable arrangements for temporary disconnection or redirection of statements.

Selling or letting your home

There are many variables here; you may be selling your house before you leave or may intend to rent it out. If you are renting it try to arrange for someone to keep an eye on the property for you. Your best bet would probably be to put it in the hands of an accommodation agency as then you will not have to worry. Some mortgage companies, though, do not take kindly to your letting your property. Some simply disallow it and others insist on very expensive insurance. Even those who are fairly amenable to the idea can take a very long time to give their approval.

Taking pets

If you are travelling to Canada for only a few months you will probably not be taking your pets. Although they can enter Canada without too much trouble, it is more difficult getting them back into Britain on your return. If your move is more permanent you may well want to take them with you. In that case you will require a certificate from a vet stating that they are in good health and fully up to date with all their vaccinations. You will also require an export licence. Your vet will be able to advise you on the current procedure.

There are several firms that specialise in relocating pets: you would be well advised to deal with them. They can advise you on all the requirements and make sure that your pet is as comfortable as possible. A partial list of these firms is in Useful Addresses. One specialist firm that also provides a very informative website is Airpets Oceanic at www.airpets.com Or you might just like to ask your vet, who may be able to advise you of a suitable local firm.

Additionally, some moving companies offer a pet travel service. Other removal companies may also offer this service; enquire when you contact them regarding your move.

Taking your car

Although it is possible to ship your car to Canada, in most cases it really isn't worth it. It will have to undergo fairly stringent testing to see if it complies with environmental and legal specifications, and will probably cost you much more than if you just sell it and buy another in Canada. You would also have the nuisance of having your steering wheel on the wrong side of the car as Canadians drive on the right.

Voting rights

You will retain your right to vote in British elections (as long as you remain a British citizen) even if you remain in Canada for some time. Contact the Electoral Registration Officer in your local district for more information. Be sure to register with the nearest British Consulate on arrival in Canada.

Taking your belongings

Not much to worry about if you are only going for a month or two. For a more permanent move, though, you will no doubt want to take considerably more of your belongings. Think about what you *really* want to take with you, as furniture is generally of good quality and not particularly expensive in Canada. You may find that your existing furniture does not fit well in the usually larger Canadian home and there is the expense of shipping it.

There are many reputable firms of international movers. Useful Addresses has a list of those contacted during the writing of this book which offered a comprehensive service to Canada. The addresses given are for their head offices; most have branches all over the country. A quick look in your *Yellow Pages* will lead to many others. Contact several firms, as charges and services vary; all should supply free quotations. It's a very competitive market, so use that to your advantage.

Customs requirements

You will be allowed to import your personal possessions into Canada without paying duty. You can get full details of your entitlements from the Canadian High Commission. Also, your removal firm may be able to provide you with the necessary forms and help you complete them, if required. It is very important to make a detailed list of all personal/household items that you are bringing with you, as well as items that may follow later. You will be required to produce two copies of this list for Customs and Immigration on arrival in Canada.

Your document checklist

As well as making all these arrangements you need to be sure to take all the official documentation you may require. Here is a short checklist of what you will need; it probably should end with 'anything else you can think of '!

Driving licence

Regulations vary from province to province, so you will need to check when you have decided on your destination. Once again, the Internet is probably your best source of up-to-date information. If you search 'driving licence' followed by your destination province you will find full details of requirements. But, wherever you are going, it is best to put the process of applying for a provincial licence in motion straight away as you will usually only be allowed to drive on your UK licence for 90 days (although some provinces are now willing to exchange a UK licence for a provincial one). The process can be time consuming and will definitely cost you. You will most likely be required to take a knowledge test (approximately C$15), road test (approximately C$50) and a vision test. In some cases you will also have to arrange a medical examination (should you be deemed to have a medical condition which could affect your ability to drive). Once that is all done, you still have to pay for a new licence, which can cost up to approximately C$75. A warning: in most provinces you will be asked to surrender your UK licence! So if you think you are likely to need that again, make a note of the number before you hand it over to facilitate replacing it on your return to the UK.

Certificates

Take all your education certificates, including any for training courses. Photocopies will not be sufficient in some cases. You will also need to take originals of such documents as birth certificate, marriage licence, certificates of adoption and so on.

References

As mentioned elsewhere, it is a very good idea to gather as many written business and personal references as you can before you leave. It is not easy for a prospective employer to telephone a referee in the UK. The same applies to landlords, who often require personal references. So get everyone you can think of to write something nice about you. When you show these recommendations in Canada make sure you keep the original.

Medical records

Visit your doctor before you leave and ask for some sort of basic record of immunisations, hospitalisations, allergies, etc. Get something similar from your dentist, and give these to your new doctor and dentist in Canada.

Passport

Be sure you have a full current passport. It's also a good idea to renew your passport if it is due to expire in the next few months – it's simply easier to do so whilst in the UK. Passport application and renewal forms are available from main post offices.

Visas

Make sure you have your visa tucked away safely with your passport as you will need to show it on arrival.

Permanent Resident Card (PRC)

It is now mandatory for all Permanent Residents to have a Permanent Residence Card (PRC). This is a small identity card carrying your name, photo and encoded information regarding your immigration status. No secure information is printed on the card. See Figure 15. The PRC was introduced by the Canadian government in 2002:

Fig. 15. Sample permanent resident card.

- to increase border security;
- to improve the integrity of the immigration process; and
- to provide holders with secure proof of their permanent residence status when re-entering Canada on a commercial carrier (plane, train, boat and bus).

A PRC is issued automatically to new Permanent Residents and the cost is included in your application for permanent residence fee. The card will be delivered to you by mail within 30 days of your entry into Canada.

Thinking about your move

Even if you have visited Canada before, or have friends or relatives there, there will inevitably be a period of readjustment. For a time it might all seem a bit confusing. Some of this disorientation can be avoided by finding out as much about your destination as possible. As well as looking at some of the publications and books listed in the Further Reading section at the end of this book (many of which you will be able to find in your local library), a visit to the Centre for International Briefing in Surrey might be worthwhile. There you will find a very good library containing all sorts of information on lifestyle, conventions, regulations and laws in various countries. They do charge a fee. And, once again, the Internet is an excellent resource.

Moving Publications Ltd is another useful source of information on specific areas of Canada. They publish a series of magazines targeted at people relocating to eight major areas in Canada, with information about real estate, cost of living, utility costs, municipal laws, transportation, education, pretty much everything you could need! The guides cover Alberta, Vancouver and BC, Montreal, Ottawa/Hull, Winnipeg and Manitoba, Toronto and Area, Saskatchewan, Greater Hamilton and Area. These can be obtained from *Canada News*.

TAKING CARE OF ESSENTIALS

Finding accommodation

Your first concern on arrival will be accommodation. If you are fortunate you will have friends or relatives who will put you up for a while. If you have been transferred by your UK firm they may have arranged accommodation for you. Failing that you will need to have sorted something out for at least the first week or so.

Locating temporary accommodation

Bed and breakfast type accommodation is available in most towns and cities and might be your best bet on arrival. Better still, arrange it before you leave. Contact the Better Business Bureau in the city or the city nearest the area you are moving to. See Useful Addresses for a list of the bureaux in major cities as well as other sources of short-term accommodation. There are quite a few websites listing bed and breakfast accommodation across Canada, and by area. Two to try are www.canadaguesthouse.com and www.bbcanada.com There are lots more – just type bed and breakfast Canada into your search engine.

Locating permanent accommodation

Once you have a temporary roof over your head you could contact a rental agency to get something more permanent. That's where the letters of recommendation you brought with you will be useful as landlords are very keen to have some evidence of your reliability before letting the accommodation. You will also need to be prepared to pay at least one month's rent in advance, as well as a security deposit usually equivalent to one month's rent in the case of furnished accommodation. After that you may wish to begin looking for a house to buy. The procedure is much the same as in the UK, except that agents tend to cover a much wider area in Canada, where they are called **real estate agents**. You will also find that you get a more comprehensive service from your agent, who will usually accompany you to homes that you wish to view and will be able to provide you with a good deal of information about the property before you see it. Although this varies from province to province, you are likely to need at least a 5 per cent deposit, in most cases 10 per cent.

Making health care provision

Heath care is another provincially regulated area. The provincial medical insurance cover in Canada is good, but it is very important to remember that in most provinces you and your family will not be eligible for cover for 90 days. Be aware that normal holiday travel insurance will not be sufficient to cover your waiting period. Canadian Immigration authorities advise you to obtain travel insurance before leaving home to cover you for two to three weeks. Once you arrive in Canada you should arrange further coverage for the interim period. Should you wish to consult an expert on this, contact:

Canadasure
2 St Marys Court
Carleton Forehoe
Norwich NR9 4AL
email: info@canadasure.com

Of course, you may choose to retain private insurance. In this case you will need to find out if the policy you currently hold will be applicable whilst you are in Canada.

Adequate travel insurance is essential if you are only going to be in Canada temporarily.

You should also find a doctor and dentist as soon as possible. These are listed in *Yellow Pages* under Physicians and Surgeons, Dentists, and Clinics-Medical. If you have friends or relatives in the area ask for recommendations. Be sure to ask if the doctor belongs to a provincial health insurance plan. If not, you will pay a great deal more for your health care. You should also compare the rates charged by dentists, as there is no universal dental insurance, although many employers offer a group plan. Take the records you brought with you from your UK doctor and dentist to your new practitioners.

CASE STUDY

Even Samantha doesn't always get it right!

It looks as if Sam has everything under control: she has upgraded her qualifications and even secured a Canadian job before leaving England. She has tidied up her affairs in the UK, arranged temporary accommodation in Vancouver and now arrives in Canada.

On the way from the airport to her bed and breakfast the taxi is involved in a slight accident. No one is seriously hurt, but Sam has bumped her head and the taxi driver insists on driving her to hospital, just to check for concussion.

'You have got travel insurance, haven't you?' asks the taxi driver.

'No. I understood I'd be covered by the BC Medicare Programme,' replies Samantha.

'Not until you've registered with the Plan,' says the receptionist in accident and emergency.

As a Permanent Resident Samantha is not instantly covered by provincial medical insurance. She needs to complete all the necessary forms and, in most provinces including BC, wait for 90 days before coverage begins. She should have arranged some temporary insurance.

Transportation

Most cities are fairly well served by public transport, but Canadians do rely on their cars pretty heavily, particularly in more rural areas. Unless you are in a big city you should probably think about getting some sort of personal transport as quickly as possible, otherwise your job search may be hampered. Car lots proliferate in most areas and good deals are to be had on second-hand cars.

REGISTERING WITH SOCIAL SECURITY

Another top priority. Although you have a work permit you will not be able to start employment without a Social Insurance Number (SIN). *Yellow Pages* again: your local Canada Human Resources and Skills Development Centre will be found under the Government Services listing. It's a pretty straightforward process: you just fill in a few forms outlining your work background, and some personal details, and you are then issued with an SIN card

Fig. 16. Sample Social Insurance Number card.

(see Figure 16 for an example). Be sure to take this with you when you attend interviews.

As well as being the place where you register for your SIN, the Canada Human Resources and Skills Development Centre is an extremely good source of information and assistance during your job search. It offers the services of government advisers, has extensive job listings and a wealth of publications, directories and lists that you can make good use of.

FINDING OUT WHERE TO LOOK

You are now set up and ready to begin the job search in earnest. Where to look? It is all a lot easier now that you are actually in your chosen locality. As mentioned you can get help from the Canada Human Resources and Skills Development Centre.

Reading the local papers

The next step is to get hold of all the local papers, both daily and weekly, and scan the jobs section. Figure 17 shows examples from several major cities. Make it your priority every day to scan these advertisements and get your applications off as quickly as possible. Sometimes a job advertisement will invite you to ring for an informal chat about the position. Do so. Anything that helps to make you memorable is to the good, and this gives a proactive impression.

Making speculative approaches

The procedure is not very different from conducting the search from the UK – just easier. Consult *Yellow Pages* for firms which seem to be in your field and send them all a speculative letter. Stress your versatility and adaptability and that you are available to start immediately.

CASE STUDY

George continues his search

George and his family have settled in Toronto. As soon as they arrive George continues his search.

At the reference library he finds a wealth of contacts and information about the Toronto area, much more than he was able to get hold of while still in the UK. He consults *Matthews Media Directory* which leads him to a couple of publications specialising in the recording industry.

George puts together individualised résumés and speculative letters for the studios mentioned in these publications.

Within ten days he has been invited to three studios to chat about possibilities.

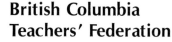
Fig. 17. Sample Canadian newspaper advertisements.

152

Using libraries

Your local library will have addresses and telephone numbers of Canadian companies arranged by job sector: for example, manufacturing, retail, service. Make use of these. Librarians are usually very keen to help, so if you let the reference librarian know what you are after and why, you will get all sorts of useful information. As in the UK the use of public libraries in Canada is free. The library will have a full selection of newspapers covering all of Canada. The Wednesday and Saturday editions usually carry the most job adverts.

Whilst in the library consult *Matthews Media Directory* for listings of daily newspapers, business and trade publications and news, satellite and wire services. Also try *Matthews CCE Directory*, containing listings for community papers, the ethnic press, multicultural radio and TV stations as well as the university newspapers and radio stations.

Some of the publications featuring job vacancy advertisements are:

- *Canada Employment Weekly*
- *Jobs, Jobs, Jobs*
- *National Business Employment Weekly.*

Finding the right publication

Job-specific magazines which carry advertisements for vacancies include:

- *CA Magazine* (for chartered accountants)
- *Canadian Music*
- *Canadian Nurse*

- *Explore*
- *Marketing Magazine*
- *Medical Post*
- *Northern Miner*
- *Pulp and Paper Canada.*

Checking the notices

Still at the library, you can check the bulletin board to find out what is available to job-seekers in your area. You might be able to:

- join a job-finding club

- offer your skills on a voluntary basis

- attend relevant lectures and job fairs

- join a professional development association.

By doing any of these you begin to immerse yourself in the community and create your own network of contacts.

Finding leads from other sources

If you have friends or relatives in your new location they might be able to introduce you to someone from their firm, or they may have other influential contacts. Don't be afraid to ask.

Human Resources and Skills Development Canada, a government body, produces various newsletters and info sheets which can be a valuable source of information about the Canadian job market. Ask at your Canada Human Resources and Skills Development Centre.

Yet another source of contacts and information is the Canada Career Information Partnership (CCIP), a national network of government and private sector agencies which provide career and labour market information to Canadians. See Useful Addresses for contact details.

The Internet will be as useful to you once you arrive in Canada as it was when you began your preliminary search. As well as investigating all the Internet sources mentioned earlier, look out for community nets and sites in your new area.

VISITING AGENCIES

Employment agencies are the other avenue to explore. Most cities have them in abundance. Your first step is to identify those which recruit in your field of expertise, and then blitz them with your letter and résumé. Be prepared for a lot of foot-work, as most will want you to come for a personal interview before putting you on their books.

Looking for the right agencies

As in the UK some agencies are better than others. Look for those that seem to be interested in you personally. In fact, an agency that doesn't want a personal interview probably isn't going to come up with much to help you. Be sure that you let them know exactly what you are looking for: you don't want to waste your time and travelling expenses attending interviews for inappropriate jobs.

Keep up the pressure. Most agencies deal with hundreds, if not thousands, of job-seekers in a month. It is easy for a consultant to remember somebody he saw yesterday, but he may forget you if you were last in touch three weeks ago. Make it part of your routine to phone them regularly, drop into their offices if you are in the vicinity. Make yourself memorable so that they remember you when the good job comes along.

For help in finding the right agencies for you try the on-line link to Association of Cdn Search Employment & Staffing Services at www.acsess.org

CHECKLIST
Before you go you will need to:

♦ Tidy up all your administrative and personal affairs.

♦ Be sure you have original copies of all important documentation including education certificates, birth certificates, marriage licence.

♦ Contact several removal companies and get quotations. Find out exactly what services they offer and get a firm price.

♦ Get personal and business references in writing.

♦ Get evidence of your automobile insurance no-claims history.

♦ Remember passports and visas.

After you arrive in Canada you will need to:

♦ Contact a Canada Human Resources and Skills Development Centre to register for employment and get your Social Insurance Number.

- Register with the Provincial Health Plan, if you are eligible.

- Find a suitable doctor and dentist.

- Start scanning the classified ads in daily and local papers.

- Check the local *Yellow Pages* for employment agencies and possible employers.

- Send out an avalanche of applications, speculative letters and letters to employment agencies.

CASE STUDY

Lucy is off to a good start

Lucy's aunt meets her plane. She is thrilled finally to be in Canada (even if she can't see much in the way of wide open spaces around the Ottawa airport!).

'We'll stop at Bob's Burger Bar on the way home, Lucy,' says her aunt. 'He's anxious to meet you. I hope it's not too much of a rush, but he's kind of hoping you could start tomorrow. They're rushed off their feet.'

'Okay,' Lucy replies. 'But I also want to call the BUNAC office. I want to travel around a bit and they may have some leads for me.'

Lucy is doubly fortunate in having the support services provided by BUNAC as well as a relative to help her on arrival.

POINTS TO CONSIDER

1. There are a lot of details to take care of before you go. Make a list of everyone you deal with on a non-personal basis (banks, hire purchase companies, tax authorities, etc). Who needs to be informed of your move? What information will they need from you? Compile your own checklist and work steadily through it.

2. Do you have all the documentation you need to take with you? Is anything missing? What will you need to send for?

3. Who could provide you with a written letter of recommendation? Consider employers and friends. Have you done any voluntary or community work in the past?

4. What do you need to do to prepare for your arrival? Have you arranged satisfactory temporary accommodation?

5. How will you arrange your job search once you arrive at your destination? You might devise a daily schedule with a list of priorities.

7

Applying for Jobs

DECIDING ON AN ANGLE

Once you have located a job possibility you still have to compete with many other suitable applicants. You have to stand out from the crowd and that means finding an angle.

Finding your assets

You already have an advantage in that you may be the only recent immigrant applying. With the great influx of immigrants to Canada that is not always the case, but it will at least make you different from the majority of the applicants. Is that your angle? If you can't come up with anything else it is better than nothing. Remember, though, that you will need to convince the prospective employer that you are likely to hang around for a while. A degree of commitment to Canada must be demonstrated. (Except for temporary or vacation work.)

It can be very effective to point out to the employer how your UK or other experience can be put to good use in the new job. You may, for example, be trained in an area in which the British have always been admired. The service industries, education and training, nursing and engineering all fall into this category. Make a special point of this when submitting your application.

Or perhaps your prospective employer is specifically looking for someone who is dynamic and forward thinking. It wouldn't take much to convince a recruiter that someone who has left their homeland to live many miles away in another country is pretty dynamic and not afraid to take chances!

Doing your research

Time spent on research is never wasted and can often mean the difference between landing the job or not. Your local library is a goldmine of information. If the company you are applying to is fairly large you will be able to find its annual report there. Also, check the periodical indexes for articles about that company. Other useful research tools include:

◆ *Canadian Key Business Directory*
◆ *Financial Post 100 Best Companies to Work for*
◆ *Directory of Associations in Canada*
◆ *CANTECH National Directory*
◆ *Classified Directory: A Complete Guide to Business in Canada*
◆ *Directory of Canadian Manufacturers*
◆ *Co-op Program Directory*
◆ *Magazines Career Directory*
◆ and, of course, the Internet – many companies have their own websites full of facts about their business.

PERFECTING THE RÉSUMÉ

In the previous chapter we looked at the differences between an English-style CV and the North American-style résumé. We also stressed the importance of tailoring your résumé to the specific job applied for. This can often simply be a question of emphasis. You can't change your experience and education but you *can* highlight the areas that make you ideal for that particular job.

Résumé of
Jean Marchand

1881 Arbutus St
Vancouver
BC V6V 1L2
tel 604 887 8865
fax 604 887 8754

JOB OBJECTIVE: Administration, Public Relations and Publishing

EMPLOYMENT

1995–2005   Editorial Assistant, *Food Science* magazine, Oxford Publishing, Oxford, UK.
Responsible for the administration of a monthly scientific journal. Maintaining, modifying and administering four databases containing information relating to articles and authors. Daily contact with authors and referees in order to achieve swift and smooth copy flow.

1993–1995   Coordinator, Southampton Women's Drop-In Centre, Southampton, UK.
Complete responsibility for administration of this government-funded society. Coordinated a 24-hour-a-day crisis phone-line in conjunction with local police. Arranged and presented lectures and courses in the community. Handled all radio, newspaper and local television interviews and articles. Supervised volunteers and participated in fund raising.

1989–1993   Secretary/Office Manager/Agent, Winsome Insurance Agency, Southampton, UK.
Responsible for all administrative aspects of running a small insurance agency, including assessing and issuing policies, as well as advising clients in my capacity of licensed insurance agent.

EDUCATION

1992   Hatfield Polytechnic, Hatfield, UK
Other Than Life Insurance Agents Licence

1985–1992   Hammersmith Secondary, London, UK
General Certificate of Education A-Levels (equivalent to post high school diploma) in English, History, Business Studies and Art.

ADDITIONAL INFORMATION

    Typing speed: 60 words per minute
Audio typing and shorthand experience
Driving licence (BC)
Computer skills: Word, Access, Excel, Publisher, Powerpoint, CorelDraw
Email and internet applications

References available on request.

Fig. 18. Generic résumé.

JOB ADVERTISEMENT FROM THE *VANCOUVER SUN*

Fund Raiser
Event Co-ordinator – Surrey

Training and/or experience in non-profit organizations specifically: (1) fund raising, including gaming (2) Coordinating fund raising events & (3) supervising volunteers & familiarity with the Surrey area. Position duration 1 year with possible renewal. Fax complete résumé detailing requested background and salary expectations to: 588-1234 by January 29.

Fig. 19. Specific job advertisement.

Making your résumé fit the job

Figures 18, 19 and 20 show an example of this tailoring. Figure 18 is a 'generic' résumé. From it you will see that Jean Marchand has a fairly wide range of administrative experience, from insurance work to public relations to fund raising. Figure 19 is the newspaper advertisement for the job she is interested in. Note that Jean has some of the experience required but fails to meet the specification of familiarity with the local area. Her relevant experience with non-profit making organisations comprises only a very small part of her career to date.

Figure 20 shows how she tweaked her résumé to highlight her suitability for this particular position and minimise the areas in which she could be seen to fall short. There wasn't a great deal Jean could do about the lack of local area knowledge; she will have to hope her other qualifications outweigh that disadvantage. As the advertisement didn't mention any requirements for administrative/secretarial experience, that aspect of her career was played down in favour of highlighting the experience at the women's centre. Even that has been modified to emphasise those

Résumé of
Jean Marchand

1881 Arbutus St
Vancouver
BC V6V 1L2
tel 604 887 8865
fax 604 887 8754

JOB OBJECTIVE: Event Coordinator/Fund Raiser

EMPLOYMENT

1995–2005   Editorial Assistant, *Food Science* magazine, Oxford Publishing, Oxford, UK.
Responsible for the administration of a monthly scientific journal. Database administration and management. Daily contact with authors. Supervision of part-time clerical help.

1993–1995   Coordinator, Southampton Women's Drop-In Centre, Southampton, UK.
Complete responsibility for administration of this government-funded society. Coordinated various fund raising events including successful dinners, entertainment evenings and raffles. Arranged and presented lectures and courses in the community and approached local companies with requests for funding assistance. Liaison with local media including radio and television interviews and press releases. Coordinated volunteer recruitment and supervised activities for volunteers.

1989–1993   Secretary/Office Manager/Agent, Winsome Insurance Agency, Southampton, UK.
Responsible for all administrative aspects of running a small insurance agency. Advising clients in my capacity of licensed insurance agent. Supervision of clerical help.

EDUCATION

1992   Hatfield Polytechnic, Hatfield, UK
Other Than Life Insurance Agents Licence

1985–1992   Hammersmith Secondary, London, UK
General Certificate of Education A-Levels (equivalent to post high school diploma) in English, History, Business Studies and Art.

ADDITIONAL INFORMATION

Typing speed: 60 words per minute
Audio typing and shorthand experience
Driving licence (BC)
Computer skills: Word, Access, Excel, Publisher, Powerpoint, CorelDraw
Email and internet applications
Past President of Kidlington Amateur Dramatic Society
Volunteer Campaigner for Heart Foundation

Fig. 20. Tailored résumé.

elements mentioned in the advertisement: fund raising and volunteer supervision. A couple of points have been added under Additional Information that are relevant to the sort of job advertised. Jean's cover letter will do even more to bring her relevant experience to the recruiter's attention.

CASE STUDIES

Samantha makes her mark

Sam has now been in Vancouver for a month and has settled in well to her new job and new way of life. Not for her the uncertainty of applying for jobs; she is lucky to have found one before she left England. However, one day she looks on the staff noticeboard and learns that a position senior to hers has just become vacant. She decides to apply for it.

Samantha has a look at her CV and realises that it does not conform to the résumé style expected in Canada. It also does not mention her recent experience. She asks to use a friend's computer and turns her CV into a résumé.

'That notice specified they wanted someone "not afraid of a challenge",' her friend observes. 'That certainly applies to you!'

'Why do you say that?'

'Well, you have just crossed the Atlantic and one entire continent to start work in a new country. You should point that out in your letter.'

Samantha refers to her move as a challenge in her covering letter.

She is delighted when, one week later, she is called to interview.

George makes the change

George is nervous of his decision to try for a bit of a career move. He has not worked in a recording studio before.

'But you did do that volunteer work in the hospital sorting out their broadcast equipment,' his wife reminds him.

'And I did an extra year's training in audio electronics.'

George needs to highlight this experience in his 'tweaked' résumé. This will draw attention to his suitability for work in a recording studio, rather than emphasise any lack of experience.

WRITING THE PERFECT COVERING LETTER

It is debatable which is more important – the résumé or the covering letter. Certainly it is in the covering letter that your personality can show through, as well as your enthusiasm. This is where you sell yourself.

Making the right connections

Think about what you are trying to get across to the recruiter. Your aim should be to convince her/him that it is worth having a closer look at your résumé. More than that, you want the recruiter to decide that you are worth interviewing, that you have something tangible to offer that company. The most effective way of achieving this is to make favourable comparisons wherever possible.

- Connect your career goals and past experience to the requirements of this position.

- Connect your special areas of expertise to the job specification.

- Connect your interests to the area in which the prospective employer operates. Make it obvious that you are absolutely right for the job.

Be certain that you provide all the information asked for in the job advertisement. In the example above, the employer requested salary expectations, so your covering letter should contain that information.

Essential elements

Each application is different and you will have to gear your letter to the tone and content of the job advertisement. However, there are several elements that ought to be in every cover letter you send:

- Address the letter to a person, not a position or, even worse, the dreaded Dear Sirs. If a name is not stated in the advertisement, or you are writing on spec, give the company a call and ask for the name of the personnel manager.

- Always name the position you are applying for. Personalise your letter wherever possible. Nobody likes to receive a form letter.

- Mention any documents you are enclosing with your application such as résumé, references. This demonstrates an organised approach as well as drawing them to the recruiter's attention.

◆ Be as specific as possible when outlining your suitability. It is better to say that you have experience of several named software programmes than make the blanket statement that you are computer literate.

◆ Say why you want the job and why you think you could do it well. Don't leave it up to the reader to make that connection – they may not!

◆ Indicate interest in the company and the area in which they work.

◆ Conclude your letter optimistically. 'I look forward to hearing from you soon' or 'I would be pleased to attend for an interview at a mutually convenient time'. This rounds off your communication in a confident and pleasant manner.

Taking those factors into consideration, how would our hopeful Event Coordinator word her letter?

◆ There is no name or telephone number given in the job advertisement. It would be worth Jean's while to send a fax stating that she is interested in the position and asking if there is anyone in particular to whom she should address her reply.

◆ Jean knows the title of the job she is applying for, so she should include this in her opening sentence.

◆ Jean has some references that are particularly relevant to this position and so has decided to include them in her application. These, and the enclosed résumé, should be mentioned in her letter.

◆ She has experience in most of the areas specified in the advertisement. She should draw the recruiter's attention to this and stress the similarity between what she did at the women's centre and the requirements of the advertised position.

◆ Jean should stress how much she enjoyed her work for the charity organisation in Southampton and why she would like to work in this sort of environment again.

◆ The advertisement asked for details of salary expectations, so this must be included in Jean's letter. That can be an awkward area, as whilst you don't want to blow your chances completely by expecting more than they are willing to pay, you don't want to undervalue your skills or leave yourself open to a low offer. The best way around this is to give a fairly wide range that starts just a bit above the minimum you are willing to accept and goes up to the highest you could reasonably hope for, based on your experience and any knowledge you have of the industry norms. Refer again to the International Pay and Benefits Survey. Many job advertisements do give salaries, so make a note of those for which you are qualified. This will give you a good idea of what you should be aiming for.

Jean's covering letter (or in this case covering fax) is shown in Figure 21.

MAXIMISING YOUR ASSETS

As the song says, 'Accentuate the positive, eliminate the negative'. This advice is applicable throughout the job-hunting process, from initial contact to final interview. What are your assets?

1881 Arbutus St
Vancouver
BC V6V 1L2
tel 604 887 8865
fax 604 887 8754
email: jean@spico

11 January 200X

Helen Ruffel
Surrey Community Centre
1435 East Road
Surrey
BC V5B 6J2

FAX: 588 8697

Dear Ms Ruffel

I am writing to apply for the position of Fund Raiser/Event Coordinator, as advertised in the Vancouver Sun. This is an exciting opportunity and one which I would be very pleased to be considered for. As you will see from the enclosed résumé, I have had considerable experience of fund raising and working with volunteers, as Coordinator of the Southampton Women's Centre. I note that your advertisement specifies experience of fund raising by gaming. One of the most successful fund raising campaigns we ran at the Women's Centre was a monthly bingo evening. Additionally, I have coordinated raffles, tombolas and similar events.

I have taken this opportunity to include some written references that I think you will find relevant to this position, including several personal references from some of the volunteers I recruited and worked with.

I'm sure you will not fail to notice that my career to date has been in the UK. I recently obtained Permanent Resident Status and arrived in Vancouver two weeks ago. I have to admit it is a city I have fallen in love with and I look forward to making my home here. It would be wonderful if my career could move back into the field of charity organisations, as my work in this area was most enjoyable and rewarding.

With regard to salary expectations, I am looking for appointments in the region of $XX,000 to $XX,000.

I look forward to hearing from you and would be pleased to meet at any convenient time to discuss the position further.

Yours sincerely

Jean Marchand

encs

Fig. 21. Sample covering letter.

- ◆ spirit of adventure
- ◆ eager for new experience
- ◆ adaptability
- ◆ ability to organise
- ◆ not afraid of big challenges.

Surely all of these are applicable to anyone intrepid enough to consider working in a new country. So point them out.

CASE STUDY

Lucy gets restless

Although grateful for the job waiting for her at the Burger Bar, Lucy is keen to see more of Canada. Metropolitan Ottawa doesn't really suit her – she still longs for those wide open spaces.

She knows that BUNAC works with the Students Working Abroad Programme (SWAP) and calls their office in Toronto to see if they have any leads. She is told of a need for clerical help in a provincial forest fire-fighting department. Applicants are invited to phone for an informal chat.

Lucy calls the number given and has an in-depth conversation with the recruiter, who is very impressed by her enthusiasm. Lucy asks lots of questions about the trees, conservation techniques, etc. The recruiter makes a note to place Lucy on the shortlist for interview.

Thinking about your personal assets

You will have your own special assets to add to this list. In fact making a list is a good idea. Decide what aspects of your character and experience show you in the best light and figure out ways to bring them into every letter, every résumé you send out, every conversation with a prospective employer. Don't be afraid of repeating yourself. The Canadian employer is used to this sort of approach and is more likely to think that the self-effacing candidate has something to hide than to applaud his reticence.

Flexibility is very important in the Canadian job market. Jobs tend to be somewhat less structured than you may be used to and you could well be expected to 'muck in' as the occasion demands, particularly in a smaller firm. Once again, someone making the move to a different country is nothing if not flexible. Remind the prospective employer of that.

Eliminating the negative

Whilst you must be seen to be keen on your new country, you should avoid any negative references to the old one or your job experiences there. Indeed, avoid all negative references completely. Concentrate on the positive aspects of your move, how your different experience could give an employer a vital edge and how keen you are to put all the knowledge that you have gained to work for them.

MAKING YOURSELF MEMORABLE

A technique used in sales is to focus on some unique aspect of your character or appearance and mention that repeatedly. The idea is that the customer (in your case the prospective employer) will remember you when making a decision regarding his purchase (appointment). That is not so easy when your first communications are all written, but it can be done. Again, you have the advantage of being distinctive as a foreigner. You can use that to make the recruiter remember you. You will, of course, have mentioned your Permanent Resident Status or Employment

Authorisation in your cover letter (not least to reassure the recruiter that you can legally work in Canada). When you come to chase up the application with a phone call your accent will make you recognisable. It gives you a talking point, too.

Phoning the company

Follow-up phone calls in themselves are a way of getting yourself noticed. In most cases it is perfectly acceptable to give the company a call if you have not had any response to your application after a week or so. Beware, however, of the advertisement which specifically requests that you do not phone. These are becoming more frequent.

On the other hand, sometimes an advertisement will invite applicants to phone for further information or 'an informal chat'. Don't waste these opportunities to make yourself memorable. It is not possible to overstate the value of that British accent (assuming that is what you have!). It will nearly always be an immediate point in your favour.

Sending photos and references

An increasingly common practice is the inclusion of a photograph with your application. This is not the norm in Canada, nor is it unacceptable. Use your judgement. If you think there is something about your appearance that will emphasise your suitability for the job, enclose a photo. Many employers in service industries have a strong interest in what candidates look like and only consider those of an appropriate appearance.

If you have written references that relate very well to the job you are applying for, enclose copies of these at the initial application stage. Another way of getting yourself remembered.

CHECKLIST

♦ Identify an angle, something that makes you stand out from the crowd.

♦ Spend some time on your résumé. Tailor it to the specifications of each job you apply for. Highlight experience which illustrates your suitability for that position.

♦ Your covering letter is very important: it is here that you really sell yourself. Point out the experience and qualifications that make you ideal for the job. Adopt a confident approach.

♦ Make connections between your past experience and the requirements for this job. Point them out in your covering letter.

♦ Whenever possible make telephone contact with potential employers. Be careful not to do this, however, when job advertisements specifically instruct you not to phone.

♦ 'Accentuate the positive, eliminate the negative.'

POINTS TO CONSIDER

1. List your experience, qualifications and qualities that would make a prospective employer want to hire you. Put them in order of importance. How can you put these qualities across in an initial contact letter? What about in person?

2. What things have you done in the past, either at work or in leisure time, that illustrate your positive assets?

3. How can you make yourself memorable? Is there anything you can put in a cover letter that would achieve this? How about later, at the interview stage?

4. Would it be advantageous to enclose a photograph with your application?

$$8$$

Landing Your Job

PREPARING FOR INTERVIEW

Doing some research

Probably the most useful thing you can do to prepare for your interview is a bit of research about the firm. This needn't be exhaustive but could include finding out about the company's products and any competition. Anyone intending to get ahead in the Canadian workplace is expected to be an enthusiastic go-getter.

You should go armed with a knowledge of the pay scales in your field. That will not be difficult, as Canadian employers and employees tend to be pretty open about salaries and these are usually mentioned in job advertisements.

Your appearance

Generally, you should dress less formally than you would for an interview in the UK, although it depends on the type of position for which you are applying. Whereas in the UK a prospective employer will expect an interviewee to arrive in a suit or equivalent, the Canadian employer could be rather intimidated if you were to turn up in your best bib and tucker for a job in, say, a production environment. Choose an outfit that is just slightly more formal than you would expect to wear in your new job on a daily basis.

What to take with you

You may not need all the following, but best to be on the safe side:

- Social Insurance Card. Your prospective employer may want to ensure that you have completed all the formalities necessary for starting work in Canada.

- Passport. Again the employer may wish to confirm that you are qualified to work in Canada. If applicable, the Permanent Resident Status document stapled into the back of your passport will reassure him.

- Permanent Resident Card. This confirms your status and the fact that you are eligible to work in Canada.

- References. Although you will have sent relevant references with your application it is a good idea to take the originals with you. The employer is not likely to want to telephone the UK to confirm your credentials so the more written documentation you can give him the better. Take along also any character references you obtained before leaving the UK. It all helps. Figure 22 is a sample of a character reference.

- Copy of the job advertisement. Useful to refer to.

- Another copy of your resumé, again for you to refer to.

Being punctual

This next piece of advice may seem odd, but it is a fact. Canadians are discomfited if you arrive early for your interview. I don't know why but I have seen it several times. It embarrasses them to have you turn up more than five minutes before your appointment. So

George Sanders
136 West Street
Luton UK LU6 123

3 November 200X

TO WHOM IT MAY CONCERN

I have been asked to supply a character reference for Alan Morton, who has been an enthusiastic and valued member of our amateur dramatics club for the past three years. I was, of course, sorry to learn that Alan would be leaving us, but feel sure that he will do well in his new venture. To be honest, I was not surprised to learn that he was planning to move to a new country, as Alan seems to thrive on challenges and I have always found I could rely on him to come up with innovative solutions to all manner of problems.

Alan has been a real asset to our club over the years and leaves behind many friends.

Yours faithfully

George Sanders
Chairman, Luton Amateur Dramatic Society (LADS)

Fig. 22. Sample character reference letter.

take a turn around the block if necessary and report for interview at precisely the arranged time.

PRESENTING YOURSELF WELL AT THE INTERVIEW

The following list of ten interview tips was prepared and issued by the Canada Human Resources and Skills Development Centre, so we must assume that it will lead you to the sort of interview behaviour favoured by the Canadian employer.

Ten interview tips

1. Dress neatly and appropriately. Do they wear suits, or dress casually?

2. Map your route in advance so that you arrive in good time.

3. Don't smoke or chew gum.

4. Greet the interviewer with a handshake.

5. Don't sit until the interviewer sits or asks you to.

6. Be calm, poised and efficient.

7. Answer questions honestly and concisely.

8. Show enthusiasm and interest.

9. Bring copies of your résumé, letters of reference or certificates that are relevant.

10. Focus on a specific job or jobs. From an employer's point of view an applicant eager to accept 'anything' may do nothing well.

Some of those are pretty obvious but they will give you an idea of the Canadian attitude.

CASE STUDIES

Samantha turns a deficit into an asset

Samantha attends an interview for the position of senior dietitian. She has not met the interviewer before. He expresses concern that she might find working practices rather different from those she has been used to in England. As she will need to deal with both patients and management in the new position, he fears this may be a problem.

'I can see that the set-up here is different, and after being here for a while I think I've got quite a good handle on it,' Sam replies. 'But I regard that as a challenge rather than a drawback. As you can see from these references, I have worked in a variety of health care situations and I feel that adaptability is one of my strong points.'

When asked about her long-term plans, Sam does not mention that she intends to return to England in a few years' time, but instead enthuses about the lifestyle in Vancouver and how well she feels it suits her.

The interviewer, who is already impressed with her credentials, feels that Sam has the right attitude to adapt to different working practices and offers her the position.

George does his research

George Robins is asked to come for an interview at Eastern Audio, a small recording studio which supplements its trade by bulk CD duplicating. George studies the market carefully before his appointment and when asked what he feels he could contribute to the company is able to offer an informed reply.

'From what I understand, Eastern Audio doesn't have a lot of competition locally so there is ample opportunity for expansion. However, a major concern must be the falling market in CDs, due to the growth of downloading music from the Internet. I have some ideas as to how to tap into that market and have some design ideas that may interest you.'

George goes on to explain that he would be happy to put in extra time to develop those ideas and adds that he has already discussed this with his wife, who is supportive.

Eastern Audio's engineering manager is impressed with George's enthusiasm and commitment and feels he would make a useful addition to the team.

Lucy gets the wrong impression

In a heavily forested area an entire department of the provincial government is devoted solely to preventing and containing forest fires. Lucy is delighted to be asked to come and speak to the personnel manager about a clerical opening in the department. However, it soon becomes obvious that the job demands greater clerical skills than she possesses. Lucy is disappointed as the ruggedness of the area really appeals to her.

'Perhaps you would be interested in another temporary position we have,' suggests the manager. 'I'm afraid it's only for two or three weeks and it can be pretty back-breaking work. We need to get all our seedlings planted before the end of the month. And believe me, that's a lot of seedlings.'

Lucy is very happy to take on this part-time job. She reckons she doesn't mind a bit of hard work and relishes the idea of finally getting out into the great outdoors.

The information interview

There is another sort of interview: the purpose of an information interview is to have an informal talk with someone who works in the field which interests you. You attend simply to gather information, and neither party feels pressured into either asking for a job or offering one. But it can lead to openings and will provide you with the names of the people in a position to hire, as well as some inside knowledge of that particular company or field.

You must not, in these circumstances, present yourself as looking for a job. You want to find out:

◆ how the organisation works
◆ what jobs may be suitable for you
◆ what additional skills you may need
◆ how to get to talk to the person who does the hiring.

The panel interview

This is an increasingly common type of interview and can be rather daunting. Various different employers arrange to hold interviews together. Their aim is to reduce costs in time, money and human resources. What it means for you is that you are facing several interviewers at once and trying to make an impact on some or all of them. Easier said than done. The upside is that you will be making yourself known to several potential employers at once.

The key to handling these interviews is to maintain your own focus. Try to ascertain before the interview which of the interviewing employers are most likely to be interested in your skills and concentrate on communicating with their representatives. Although it is not easy (and may cause you to end the interview with a sore and spinning head!), make as much eye contact as possible with those you have identified as good potentials. When asked a question, reply mainly to the person asking it, but try to include all those present in your response.

The telephone interview

This is another form of interview that is becoming more common. Once again, it is often done to help employers cut resource costs. It is most often used as an initial interview and usually followed (if successful) by a personal meeting.

Basically, the rules here are pretty much as in a face-to-face interview. The main differences are that you cannot have eye contact and it can be difficult to maintain concentration and focus. Nevertheless, you still need to present yourself professionally and confidently. The best idea is to prepare yourself just as for a personal interview, with all relevant documents and information easily to hand. Set yourself up somewhere you will not be disturbed by family members or visitors. Have a desk or table in front of you for your papers and sit straight in your chair rather than lounge. Believe it or not, your posture can be heard in your voice.

ACCENTUATING THE POSITIVE

One of the first questions the interviewer is likely to ask is why you have moved to Canada. Make sure that your reply is positive. Don't say derogatory things about the UK or your life there as that will only establish you as a moaner. Point out instead the opportunities that are available in Canada and your own goals for improvement. Show yourself to be a go-getter. Be careful, though, not to give the impression that you are likely to flit off to pastures greener. Indicate commitment to your new life in Canada. Most Canadians are proud of their country and will be pleased that you wish to be a part of it.

The prospective employer may feel that your lack of working experience in Canada could be a disadvantage. Turn this around by pointing out that you can bring a fresh outlook and new ways of looking at things. Canadians are not averse to change for the better! Remember that most Canadians (the Anglophone ones, anyway) are attracted to things British. If you are going to be working with the public this could be a distinct advantage.

Showing you are adaptable

Draw attention to your adaptability. It is a valued trait in the Canadian job market. Many companies are small (less than 50 people) and job descriptions tend to be much less structured than you may be used to. It is often the case of everybody 'mucking in' to get the job done or the product out. This is true even in larger companies, many of which down-sized during the recession and now do not have sufficient personnel to deal with the recent rapid recovery of the economy.

NEGOTIATING TERMS

Leave

Some things such as holiday and sick leave are usually pretty inflexible, and, in general, less generous than those in the UK. Expect only about 10–15 days' allowance for sick leave and, usually, two weeks' holiday leave (known as vacation). The latter may improve after you have been some time with the company.

There are several public holidays each year and you will be entitled to these (or time off in lieu). There are two types of public holiday: the federal days apply across the whole country while each province also has its own holidays. These are outlined in Figure 23.

National

New Year's Day	
Good Friday	
Easter Monday	
Victoria Day	Monday before 25 May
Canada Day	1 July*
Labour Day	first Monday in September
Thanksgiving	second Monday in October
Remembrance Day	11 November
Christmas Day	
Boxing Day	

Provincial

Alberta
Family Day	third Monday in February
Heritage Day	first Monday in August

British Columbia
BC Day	first Monday in August

Manitoba
Civic holiday	first Monday in August

Newfoundland (holidays are usually observed on nearest Monday)
St Patrick's Day	17 March
St George's Day	23 April
Discovery Day	24 June
Memorial Day	1 July
Orangemen's Day	12 July
Regatta Day	fixed by municipal council orders

Ontario
Civic holiday	usually first Monday in August

Quebec
National Day	24 June

Saskatchewan
Civic holiday	first Monday in August

Yukon
Discovery Day	third Monday in August

Northwest Territories
Civic holiday	first Monday in August

*(or 2 July where 1 July is a Sunday)

Fig. 23. Canadian public statutory holidays.

Hours

A 35 to 40-hour working week is the norm, although this is becoming less common. Many Canadians work at one or more part-time jobs. Statistics Canada report that the number of people working part-time has doubled since 1975 to approximately 40 per cent.

You may well find yourself working considerably longer hours than those stated in your contract. This is largely due to under-staffing. You will be expected to cooperate and should eventually be rewarded with advancement within the company. This does not, of course, apply to jobs with hourly rates where overtime is paid.

Flexi-time is common, with core working hours of 10a.m. to 4p.m., but you will be expected to make up time for doctor and dentist appointments.

Pay

This is where your earlier research comes in. A small company will be more flexible on the subject of salary, whereas larger companies usually have fixed salary bands.

Working conditions

There is no overall federal policy on pay and working conditions, although each province has its own regulations. If you have any concerns contact the Employment Division in the province you have moved to, or ask the Canada Human Resources Development Centre to advise you.

Trade unions

Trade unions are active in many segments of Canadian industry. Approximately one-third of Canada's labour force belong to a trade union. See Useful Addresses for the major organisations with which almost all Canadian trades unions are affiliated.

Other things to ask about

There are various perks and incentives throughout the industries. Establish if any of these are offered:

◆ As outlined earlier, provincial health insurance schemes (Medicare) are available and very good value for money. Some employers will make your contributions, so ask about this.

◆ Dental plan. Dental treatment is not included under Medicare, but many firms have group policies.

◆ Pensions and life assurance. These benefits follow much the same pattern as in UK companies.

◆ Bonuses. As in the UK many firms offer incentive and profit-share schemes.

◆ Overtime. Enquire as to individual company policy.

STARTING YOUR NEW JOB

The first day

Take with you:

◆ National Insurance card
◆ Permanent Resident card
◆ Medical card (if your employer is going to make your contributions).

As far as dress code is concerned, follow more or less the same rules as for the interview. Be led by what you observed co-workers wearing. It is probably inevitable that you will have a tendency at first to overdress. Don't worry – they will probably see it as a charming example of English eccentricity!

Fitting in

You may find the Canadian attitude to time-keeping more laid back than you are used to. But remember that works both ways. If additional hours are required from you it is expected that you will oblige willingly and cheerfully.

A fairly informal atmosphere is likely to prevail, especially in smaller companies. Follow the lead of your co-workers when deciding whether to address superiors by their first names. You will be on first-name terms with your workmates and probably your immediate superior.

It is almost a prerequisite of work in a Canadian company that you be willing to socialise outside working hours. Many companies arrange outings, sporting events and family days. You could be considered snobbish or unfriendly if you do not join in.

A reminder about tax

Although Canadian employers deduct tax from your income at source, you will be required to complete your own return at the end of the tax year, which in Canada runs from 1 January to 31 December. So if you incur tax-deductible expenses during the course of your job make notes and keep receipts from the beginning.

CHECKLIST

◆ Find out something about the business of the company to which you are applying.

◆ Arm yourself with a good idea of salary expectations.

◆ Take your Social Insurance card, passport, Permanent Resident card and all references.

◆ Be positive. Show your enthusiasm and adaptability.

◆ Find out about benefits and incentives.

◆ Don't be too formal. Take your lead from co-workers in matters of dress and etiquette.

QUESTIONS AND ANSWERS

Now that you have that all-important interview lined up, time spent in preparation can make all the difference.

1. *What makes you right for this job?*
How can you draw on past experience to demonstrate your suitability for this particular position?

Have you worked in a similar field or undertaken other tasks of this nature?

What do you know about this sphere of business?

Do you have any ideas on how this firm could increase their performance/profitability?

2. *How does your international background make you a better candidate?*

The interviewer wants to be sure that you are committed to your new life. How can you convince him/her that you really intend to make a mark in Canada?

What are your real reasons for deciding to work in Canada?

Will these be acceptable to a prospective employer?

What differences can you see between working practices in Canada and the UK?

How would this knowledge be valuable to a prospective employer?

3. *Can you fit in to the Canadian workplace?*

Do you have an open attitude towards working hours?

Are you willing to put in extra time when required?

Are you prepared to cope with a less formal structure at work?

Does this make you uncomfortable in any way?

What are your feelings regarding socialising with colleagues outside of working hours?

Would you regard this as an imposition?

4. *What makes you memorable?*

Someone who has decided to live and work in another country already stands out from the crowd. What can you say at the interview that will emphasise this and draw attention to your adaptability?

Have you considered what the average Canadian's perception is of people of your nationality?

How can you utilise this to your advantage?

Are you willing to 'play' on your differences, should that seem appropriate?

POINTS TO CONSIDER

1. Gather together your written references. Which ones illustrate your enthusiasm and adaptability? How can you draw the interviewer's attention to these?

2. Make a list of all the possible benefits available. Which would be particularly valuable to you? Could any be used as bargaining tools in negotiation?

3. Imagine what questions the interviewer is likely to ask you. How can you formulate your answers to demonstrate a positive attitude?

9

Moving Onwards and Upwards

RECOGNISING OPPORTUNITIES

The first job you take in Canada may not be exactly what you are looking for. It's not unlike the situation when you first joined the workforce after leaving school: you need to get your foot on the ladder. The newspaper *Canada News* reported that trained professionals who immigrated to Canada were finding it difficult to compete with their Canadian counterparts, even if the immigrants' qualifications and experience were superior. A sobering thought, but not necessarily daunting: it simply becomes necessary to adopt a career strategy. You may need to accept a position lower on the professional ladder than you currently hold, but the tradition of advancement is a strong one in the Canadian workplace. Look out for the opportunities and you can soon regain your status and begin to improve on it.

Gaining advancement

The most obvious means of advancement is from within the company you are working for. That is dealt with a bit later in this chapter. Canada's economy is strong and growing and once you have made your mark your opportunities need not be limited. Keep your finger on the pulse of what is happening within your field of expertise. Keep up with Canadian politics and watch the economy. You may see a chance to make a lateral move within your field. And don't forget to keep an eye on all regions of Canada. There is a great deal going on and new opportunities arise all the time.

WEIGHING THE OPTIONS

If the chance of advancement within your company does not look promising you might consider these options.

Changing locale

Canada is a changing, growing country and opportunities you might not have previously considered can present themselves. For example, Vancouver is swiftly becoming the Hollywood of the North, with major motion pictures filmed there in whole or in part, as well as TV programmes such as *The X-Files* and *Smallville*. Is that something you might be able to take advantage of?

CASE STUDY

George makes a move

Although George did find a job in a recording studio, it was not really the sort of thing he had in mind, his real aim being to move into the actual recording side of things, rather than technical engineering.

He keeps an eye on all that is happening in the recording industry in Canada, subscribing to several professional publications and keeping his ear to the ground at work. Soon he identifies several opportunities in Vancouver. With the growth of the film industry in that province there are more and more openings for audio experts.

Whilst still retaining his job in Toronto, George begins to apply for other studio jobs, and writes several speculative letters to studios in Vancouver. Although he is relatively happy in his job he continues to work towards his final aim.

Upgrading your qualifications

Perhaps even more so than in Britain, Canadian employers are impressed by anyone keen to improve their qualifications and employability. Many Canadians regularly attend night school to enhance their job prospects. Courses are extremely varied and widely available. Look in your regional newspapers and *Yellow Pages*. The following federal government agencies dealing with occupational training may also be of help:

Employment and Immigration Canada
Public Inquiries Centre
Public Affairs Branch
Journal Tower South
365 Laurier Ave West
Hull, PQ K1A 1LI
Tel: (613) 954 9019. Fax: (613) 954 2221

Public Service Commission
Training Programs Branch
300 Laurier Ave W
Ottawa
ON K1A 0M7
Tel: (613) 992 9562. Fax: (613) 992 9352
email: infocom.psc-cfp.gc.ca

Self-employment

It is not necessarily true that all the world loves an entrepreneur, but certainly the Canadian provincial and federal governments seem to. Both are placing a great emphasis on job creation, and offer assistance and incentives to those wishing to start up a business that will create employment for other Canadians.

Municipal governments can also provide guidance. Look in your local *Yellow Pages* under Government for further information.

The Canadian Human Resources Development and Skills Centre national office recently issued a list of business opportunities that were projected to do well:

◆ health care/home care services

◆ retirement homes located in attractive small towns

◆ auto services, repair/maintenance work done in customers' driveways

◆ entertainment programming for the expanded cable networks

◆ software, software, software

◆ personal and home security systems

◆ custom clothing, including shoes especially for seniors

◆ foreign language training

◆ home office products and services

◆ environmental products to protect drinking water and assist with waste disposal

◆ low fat/low sodium foods and meats

◆ inexpensive fast food

◆ audio and visual aids for older individuals

◆ special travel opportunities for older travellers

- healthy, natural pesticide-free foods

- interactive technology, cellular phones and home theatre equipment.

You might also like to take a look at *Entrepreneur Magazine's The Complete Guide to Owning a Home-Based Business* or visit their website at www.entrepreneur.com for many other informative titles.

Other foreign opportunities

If you still have the globe-trotting urge, keep up your contacts with the ex-pat network by subscribing to publications such as *Overseas Jobs Express* and *Expatriate Magazine*. Often employers will favour a proven ex-pat who can demonstrate flexibility and the ability to adapt to new conditions.

Unemployment benefits

There is a qualifying period for the federal unemployment insurance scheme so it will only apply if you have been in work for about six months. Should you find yourself unemployed after a period of work in Canada, head to the Human Resources Development and Skills Centre and sign on for UIC. UIC stands for Unemployment Insurance Commission, which is the government body administering the system, but the benefits themselves are also referred to as UIC.

RISING WITHIN THE COMPANY

The potential for upward movement in the Canadian workplace is good. Show yourself to be a go-getter. Identify areas where expansion is possible and let it be known that you would like to be a part of that growth.

Establishing your reputation

If your company is large enough to have a personnel or human resources department make certain that the officers are informed of your career goals. In a smaller company you should make your immediate superior and possibly his boss aware of your aims. If you are willing to relocate be sure to let them know. If you are interested in training for new areas within the company they should be aware of this also. It will do you no harm to get a reputation as someone who is keen to advance and willing to accommodate change.

If you do take any courses to improve your position, inform your employer. Try to make it plain how your increased knowledge would be of use to their company.

Research can be a valuable tool. Find out all you can about the company you are working for and the marketplace. If you can identify an area for expansion let your employer know how you could play a part. Even if that falls through you will be seen as dynamic.

You may be well placed for any relocations available within your company as you have already demonstrated that you are able to make a major move and adapt to new conditions. If any such positions arise, emphasise your experience.

UTILISING YOUR EXPERIENCE

If you had to take a step down the corporate or professional ladder, perhaps because your professional qualifications did not translate well into the Canadian market, don't let it stop you. Contact The Canadian Information Centre for International

Credentials to find out what you need to do to gain the necessary accreditation. Often it will only be a matter of taking an examination or doing a short course. Sometimes you will need to have a certain amount of Canadian experience.

Searching for a job in a new country can be a daunting experience, but you have done it successfully. In the course of your search you will have identified many sources of information and channels through which to find a job. Should you decide on a change, take advantage of the knowledge you have gained and start a campaign on much the same lines. This time you will have the added advantage of Canadian work experience.

RETURNING HOME

There are three main reasons why you might leave Canada and return home.

You have completed a temporary/vacation job or exchange visit

This is pretty straightforward. You will have taken only necessary possessions with you, so it is probably just a case of packing a couple of large suitcases and getting on a prearranged flight. If you have opened any accounts during your stay make sure these are cleared or you have made arrangements for payment. Remember to collect any relevant references from your Canadian employers.

You were temporarily relocated to Canada by your UK employer

The circumstances are going to vary greatly when a secondment is completed, but in most cases a great deal of the necessary arrangements will be made by your employer. It is up to you, however, to clear up all personal details such as credit payments.

Personal reasons necessitate a return

There could be many different reasons why you feel you have to leave Canada, from having to return home to care for an elderly parent to having tried it and not liked it. If the latter is the case it is important that you adopt a good attitude toward the situation, not look on the venture as a failure. You made the move, you got a job in a foreign country and made a home there. Now you have assessed your situation and decided that you prefer your home country. That is perfectly acceptable.

It is going to be almost as complex and exhausting moving back home as it was leaving in the first place. You do not have to worry about work permits, immigration status or learning about the country, but you will need to make all the same arrangements regarding paying off creditors, dealing with income tax, selling your house and car, engaging movers. There is the question of a job back home. Do the same as you did when you started your venture and begin your job search before you leave. First step might be to contact your last UK employer. Get relatives and friends to send you the jobs section of various British newspapers. Start contacting international and UK recruitment agencies.

CASE STUDIES

Samantha goes home

Although she thoroughly enjoyed her three years in Canada Sam is now ready to return to England. She is concerned about her mother, who is getting a bit frail and, in any case, she had no intention of making Canada her home for good. She ties up all the loose ends in Canada and heads back to the UK. There she finds some people's attitude difficult.

'So, couldn't hack it, huh?'

'Weren't the streets paved with gold after all?'

'I'm sorry it didn't work out.'

Patiently but firmly, Sam explains that her time in Canada was an adventure and that she thoroughly enjoyed it but felt it was time to return home for many reasons. She emphasises how glad she is to have had the Canadian experience. In so doing she ensures that no one, herself included, perceives her return home as a failure.

Lucy gets the travel bug

After her foray into forestry Lucy is ready for anything. She has gained a new confidence and is willing to try all sorts of challenges. In the next few months she works as a ride attendant at an amusement park in Vancouver, a waitress in a remote café in Alberta and a housekeeper (chambermaid) in several hotels across Canada.

She loves every minute of it and is sorry when the time comes to return to Britain. Although keen to complete her degree, she can't wait to see more of the world. And she knows that she will return to Canada, as it turned out to be all she hoped it would.

Permanent Resident Status

A word of warning. Your Permanent Resident Status becomes invalid if you make your home outside Canada for any great length of time. This is referred to as abandoning Canada as your place of residence, and defined as having frequent and/or lengthy absences from Canada.

SIGNING OFF

The title of this final chapter could be applied to the whole adventure, from making your decision to work in Canada, achieving the necessary immigration permissions, deciding where to work, finding the right job and settling in.

The preceding pages contain a great deal of information about how to achieve your goal. The rest of the book outlines that information in an easy-to-find format. I hope that it will be helpful and that you enjoy your Canadian experience. The Canadian way of life is both unique and rewarding. Although there may appear to be many similarities between the UK and Canada, at times the differences can seem as vast as the country itself. Even the common language is not always the same. Many everyday items are known by completely different names. For example, a biscuit is a cookie and a cracker is a biscuit! Your car does not have a bonnet and a boot, but a hood and a trunk.

As well as the changes in vocabulary, the Canadian accent can take some getting used to. Although far from universal, the rising inflection at the end of sentences and the frequent use of 'eh?' is something you will soon become used to hearing. On that note you may appreciate the following description of how Canada was named.

Three early settlers – Dave, Bill and George – were sitting around the campfire one evening congratulating themselves on having found such a plentiful and pleasant land. They were, however, concerned that their new home was as yet un-named. Dave suggested that they put letters of the alphabet into a hat

and draw them out at random until a suitable name suggested
itself. This they did. Digging deep into the hat each of the
three settlers drew out a letter. And thus Canada was named.

Dave: I got a 'C', eh?'

Bill: I got an 'N', eh?'

George: I got a 'D', eh?'

Good luck, eh!

CHECKLIST

♦ Be prepared to take a step down on the career ladder, but be
aware of how you can recover that lost ground.

♦ Find out what you can do to upgrade your qualifications and/
or translate them into Canadian equivalents.

♦ Be on the lookout for advancement within your company.
Make sure that your employers are aware of your career goals.

♦ Consider the option of self-employment.

♦ Your chances of career advancement could be improved by
embarking on further training.

♦ Keep your finger on what is happening with the Canadian
economy. Be on the lookout for opportunities.

♦ If you decide to return home clear up as many loose ends as
possible before you leave. If possible set your job search in
motion before leaving Canada.

POINTS TO CONSIDER

1. You will have become aware of many avenues for job searches. Which of these will remain relevant once you have landed a job? Would it be worthwhile to keep up any subscriptions?

2. How much do you know about the economic growth of Canada? How could you best keep abreast of events that are relevant to your field?

3. Consider the option of further training to improve your chances of promotion. What courses are available to you locally? Do any interest you on a personal as well as a career level? Which would be most impressive to your current or prospective new employer?

4. If you are leaving Canada, what references can you gather that will be helpful to you back home?

National Occupations Classification List

The following occupations are listed in Skill Type 0, Skill Level A or B of the National Occupation Classification List.

Code	A
0632	Accommodation Service Managers
5135	Actors and Comedians
1221	Administrative Officers
0114	Administrative Services Managers (other)
0312	Administrators – Post-Secondary Education and Vocational
2146	Aerospace Engineers
2222	Agricultural and Fish Products Inspectors
8252	Agricultural and Related Service Contractors and Managers
2123	Agricultural Representatives, Consultants and Specialists
2271	Air Pilots, Flight Engineers and Flying Instructors
2272	Air Traffic Control and Related Occupations
2244	Aircraft Instrument, Electrical and Avionics Mechanics, Technicians and Inspectors
7315	Aircraft Mechanics and Aircraft Inspectors
3234	Ambulance Attendants and Other Paramedical Occupations
5231	Announcers and Other Broadcasters
8257	Aquaculture Operators and Managers
2151	Architects
2251	Architectural Technologists and Technicians
0212	Architecture and Science Managers
5113	Archivists
5244	Artisans and Craftpersons
1235	Assessors, Valuators and Appraisers
5251	Athletes
5225	Audio and Video Recording Technicians
3141	Audiologists and Speech-Language Pathologists
5121	Authors and Writers
7321	Automotive Service Technicians, Truck Mechanics and Mechanical Repairers
Code	**B**
6252	Bakers
0122	Banking, Credit and Other Investment Managers
2221	Biological Technologists and Technicians
2121	Biologists and Related Scientists
7266	Blacksmiths and Die Setters
7262	Boilermakers
1231	Bookkeepers
7281	Bricklayers
5224	Broadcast Technicians
4163	Business Development Officers and Marketing Researchers and Consultants
0123	Business Services Managers (other)
6251	Butchers and Meat Cutters – Retail and Wholesale

Code	C
7272	Cabinetmakers
7247	Cable Television Service and Maintenance Technicians
3217	Cardiology Technologists
7271	Carpenters
9231	Central Control and Process Operators, Mineral and Metal Processing
6241	Chefs
2134	Chemical Engineers
2211	Chemical Technologists and Technicians
2112	Chemists
3122	Chiropractors
2231	Civil Engineering Technologists and Technicians
2131	Civil Engineers
6215	Cleaning Supervisors
5252	Coaches
4131	College and Other Vocational Instructors
7382	Commercial Divers
0643	Commissioned Officers, Armed Forces
0641	Commissioned Police Officers
4212	Community and Social Service Workers
0213	Computer and Information Systems Managers
2281	Computer and Network Operators and Web Technicians
2147	Computer Engineers (except Software Engineers)
2174	Computer Programmers and Interactive Media Developers
7282	Concrete Finishers
5132	Conductors, Composers and Arrangers
1226	Conference and Event Planners
2224	Conservation and Fishery Officers
5112	Conservators and Curators
2234	Construction Estimators
2264	Construction Inspectors
0711	Construction Managers
7311	Construction Millwrights and Industrial Mechanics (except Textile)
7215	Contractors and Supervisors, Carpentry Trades
7212	Contractors and Supervisors, Electrical Trades and Telecommunications
7217	Contractors and Supervisors, Heavy Construction Equipment Crews
7216	Contractors and Supervisors, Mechanic Trades
7214	Contractors and Supervisors, Metal Forming, Shaping and Erecting Trades
7219	Contractors and Supervisors, Other Construction Trades, Installers, Repairers
7213	Contractors and Supervisors, Pipefitting Trades
6242	Cooks
1227	Court Officers and Justices of the Peace
1244	Court Recorders and Medical Transcriptionists
7371	Crane Operators
1236	Customs, Ship and Other Brokers
Code	D
5134	Dancers
2172	Database Analysts and Data Administrators
2273	Deck Officers, Water Transport

3222	Dental Hygienists and Dental Therapists
3223	Dental Technologists, Technicians and Laboratory
3113	Dentists
3221	Denturists
3132	Dietitians and Nutritionists
2253	Drafting Technologists and Technicians
7372	Drillers and Blasters D Surface Mining, Quarrying and Construction
6214	Dry Cleaning and Laundry Supervisors
Code	**E**
4214	Early Childhood Educators and Assistants
4162	Economists and Economic Policy Researchers and Analysts
5122	Editors
4166	Education Policy Researchers, Consultants and Program Officers
4143	Educational Counsellors
7332	Electric Appliance Servicers and Repairers
2241	Electrical and Electronics Engineering Technologists and Technicians
2133	Electrical and Electronics Engineers
7333	Electrical Mechanics
7244	Electrical Power Line and Cable Workers
7241	Electricians (except Industrial and Power System)
3218	Electroencephalographic and Other Diagnostic Technologists, n.e.c.
2242	Electronic Service Technicians (Household and Business)
7318	Elevator Constructors and Mechanics
4213	Employment Counsellors
2274	Engineer Officers, Water Transport
2262	Engineering Inspectors and Regulatory Officers
0211	Engineering Managers
1222	Executive Assistants
6213	Executive Housekeepers
Code	**F**
0721	Facility Operation and Maintenance Managers
4153	Family Marriage and Other Related Counsellors
8253	Farm Supervisors and Specialized Livestock Workers
8251	Farmers and Farm Managers
5222	Film and Video Camera Operators
1112	Financial and Investment Analysts
1111	Financial Auditors and Accountants
0111	Financial Managers
1114	Financial Officers (other)
0642	Fire Chiefs and Senior Firefighting Officers
6262	Firefighters
8261	Fishing Masters and Officers
8262	Fishing Vessel Skippers and Fishermen/women
7295	Floor Covering Installers
6212	Food Service Supervisors
2122	Forestry Professionals
2223	Forestry Technologists and Technicians
6272	Funeral Directors and Embalmers

Code	G
7253	Gas Fitters
2212	Geological and Mineral Technologists and Technicians
2144	Geological Engineers
2113	Geologists, Geochemists and Geophysicists
7292	Glaziers
0412	Government Managers – Economic Analysis, Policy Development
0413	Government Managers – Education Policy Development and Program Administration
0411	Government Managers – Health and Social Policy Development and Program Administration
6234	Grain Elevator Operators
5223	Graphic Arts Technicians
5241	Graphic Designers and Illustrators
Code	**H**
6271	Hairstylists and Barbers
3151	Head Nurses and Supervisors
3123	Health Diagnosing and Treating (other professional occupations)
4165	Health Policy Researchers, Consultants and Program Officers
7312	Heavy-Duty Equipment Mechanics
0112	Human Resources Managers
Code	**I**
1228	Immigration, Employment Insurance and Revenue Officers
2141	Industrial and Manufacturing Engineers
2252	Industrial Designers
7242	Industrial Electricians
2233	Industrial Engineering and Manufacturing Technologists and Technicians
2243	Industrial Instrument Technicians and Mechanics
2171	Information Systems Analysts and Consultants
2263	Inspectors in Public and Environmental Health and Occupational Health and Safety
4216	Instructors (other)
4215	Instructors and Teachers of Persons with Disabilities
7293	Insulators
1233	Insurance Adjusters and Claims Examiners
6231	Insurance Agents and Brokers
1234	Insurance Underwriters
0121	Insurance, Real Estate and Financial Brokerage Managers
5242	Interior Designers
7264	Ironworkers
Code	**J**
7344	Jewellers, Watch Repairers and Related Occupations
5123	Journalists
4111	Judges
1227	Justices of the Peace
Code	**L**
2254	Land Survey Technologists and Technicians
2154	Land Surveyors
2225	Landscape and Horticultural Technicians and Specialists
2152	Landscape Architects
8255	Landscaping and Grounds Maintenance Contractors and Managers

4112	Lawyers and Quebec Notaries
1242	Legal Secretaries
0011	Legislators
5111	Librarians
5211	Library and Archive Technicians and Assistants
0511	Library, Archive, Museum and Art Gallery Managers
3233	Licensed Practical Nurses
1232	Loan Officers
8241	Logging Machinery Operators
Code	**M**
7316	Machine Fitters
7231	Machinists and Machining and Tooling Inspectors
0512	Managers – Publishing, Motion Pictures, Broadcasting and Performing Arts
0311	Managers in Health Care
0414	Managers in Public Administration (other)
0314	Managers in Social, Community and Correctional Services
0911	Manufacturing Managers
2255	Mapping and Related Technologists and Technicians
2161	Mathematicians, Statisticians and Actuaries
2232	Mechanical Engineering Technologies and Technicians
2132	Mechanical Engineers
3212	Medical Laboratory Technicians
3211	Medical Laboratory Technologists and Pathologists' Assistants
3215	Medical Radiation Technologists
1243	Medical Secretaries
3216	Medical Sonographers
3219	Medical Technologists and Technicians (other – except Dental Health)
2142	Metallurgical and Materials Engineers
2213	Meteorological Technicians
2114	Meteorologists
3232	Midwives and Practitioners of Natural Healing
2143	Mining Engineers
4154	Ministers of Religion
5226	Motion Pictures, Broadcasting (other Technical and Co-ordinating Occupations)
7322	Motor Vehicle Body Repairers
7334	Motorcycle and Other Related Mechanics
5212	Museums and Art Galleries (related Technical Occupations)
5133	Musicians and Singers
Code	**N**
4161	Natural and Applied Science Policy Researchers, Consultants and Program Officers
2261	Nondestructive Testers and Inspectors
8254	Nursery and Greenhouse Operators and Managers
Code	**O**
3143	Occupational Therapists
8232	Oil and Gas Well Drillers, Servicers, Testers and Related Workers
7331	Oil and Solid Fuel Heating Mechanics
3231	Opticians
3121	Optometrists

Code	P
7294	Painters and Decorators
5136	Painters, Sculptors and Other Visual Artists
9234	Papermaking and Coating Control Operators
4211	Paralegal and Related Occupations
5245	Patternmakers – Textile, Leather and Fur Products
5232	Performers (other)
1223	Personnel and Recruitment Officers
2145	Petroleum Engineers
9232	Petroleum, Gas and Chemical Process Operators
3131	Pharmacists
5221	Photographers
2115	Physical Sciences (other professional occupations)
3112	Physicians – General Practitioners and Family Physicians
3111	Physicians – Specialist
2111	Physicists and Astronomers
3142	Physiotherapists
7252	Pipefitters
7284	Plasterers, Drywall Installers and Finishers and Lathers
7251	Plumbers
6261	Police Officers (except commissioned)
0132	Postal and Courier Services Managers
4122	Post-Secondary Teaching and Research Assistants
7243	Power System Electricians
7352	Power Systems and Power Station Operators
0811	Primary Production Managers (except Agriculture)
7381	Printing Press Operators
4155	Probation and Parole Officers and Related Occupations
5131	Producers, Directors, Choreographers and Related Occupations
2148	Professional Engineers, n.e.c. (other)
1122	Professional Occupations in Business Services to Management
5124	Professional Occupations in Public Relations and Communications
4121	Professors – University
5254	Program Leaders and Instructors in Recreation and Sport
4168	Program Officers Unique to Government
1224	Property Administrators
4151	Psychologists
9233	Pulping Control Operators
1225	Purchasing Agents and Officers
0113	Purchasing Managers
Code	**R**
7361	Railway and Yard Locomotive Engineers
7314	Railway Carmen/women
7362	Railway Conductors and Brakemen/women
2275	Railway Traffic Controllers and Marine Traffic Regulators
6232	Real Estate Agents and Salespersons
0513	Recreation and Sports Program and Service Directors
4167	Recreation, Sports and Fitness Program Supervisors Consultants
7313	Refrigeration and Air Conditioning Mechanics

3152	Registered Nurses
4217	Religious Occupations (other)
0712	Residential Home Builders and Renovators
3214	Respiratory Therapists, Clinical Perfusionists and Cardio-Pulmonary Technologists
0631	Restaurant and Food Service Managers
6233	Retail and Wholesale Buyers
0621	Retail Trade Managers
6211	Retail Trade Supervisors
7291	Roofers and Shinglers
Code	**S**
0611	Sales, Marketing and Advertising Managers
0313	School Principals and Administrators of Elementary and Secondary
1241	Secretaries (except Legal and Medical)
1113	Securities Agents, Investment Dealers and Brokers
0012	Senior Government Managers and Officials
0013	Senior Managers − Financial, Communications and Other Business
0016	Senior Managers − Goods Production, Utilities, Transportation and Construction
0014	Senior Managers − Health, Education, Social and Community
0015	Senior Managers − Trade, Broadcasting and Other Services, n.e.c.
6216	Service Supervisors (other)
0651	Services Managers (other)
7261	Sheet Metal Workers
7343	Shoe Repairers and Shoemakers
7335	Small Engine and Equipment Mechanics (other)
4164	Social Policy Researchers, Consultants and Program Officers
4169	Social Science, n.e.c. (other professional occupations)
4152	Social Workers
2173	Software Engineers
1121	Specialists in Human Resources
5253	Sports Officials and Referees
7252	Sprinkler System Installers
7351	Stationary Engineers and Auxiliary Equipment Operators
7252	Steamfitters, Pipefitters and Sprinkler System Installers
7263	Structural Metal and Platework Fabricators and Fitters
9223	Supervisors, Electrical Products Manufacturing
9222	Supervisors, Electronics Manufacturing
9225	Supervisors, Fabric, Fur and Leather Products Manufacturing
1212	Supervisors, Finance and Insurance Clerks
9213	Supervisors, Food, Beverage and Tobacco Processing
9215	Supervisors, Forest Products Processing
9224	Supervisors, Furniture and Fixtures Manufacturing
1211	Supervisors, General Office and Administrative Support Clerks
8256	Supervisors, Landscape and Horticulture
1213	Supervisors, Library, Correspondence and Related Information Clerks
8211	Supervisors, Logging and Forestry
7211	Supervisors, Machinists and Related Occupations
1214	Supervisors, Mail and Message Distribution Occupations
9211	Supervisors, Mineral and Metal Processing
8221	Supervisors, Mining and Quarrying

7222	Supervisors, Motor Transport and Other Ground Transit Operators
9221	Supervisors, Motor Vehicle Assembling
8222	Supervisors, Oil and Gas Drilling and Service
9226	Supervisors, Other Mechanical and Metal Products Manufacturing
9227	Supervisors, Other Products Manufacturing and Assembly
9212	Supervisors, Petroleum, Gas and Chemical Processing and Utilities
9214	Supervisors, Plastic and Rubber Products Manufacturing
7218	Supervisors, Printing and Related Occupations
7221	Supervisors, Railway Transport Operations
1215	Supervisors, Recording, Distributing and Scheduling Occupations
9216	Supervisors, Textile Processing
5227	Support Occupations in Motion Pictures, Broadcasting and the Performing Arts
2283	Systems Testing Technicians
Code	**T**
7342	Tailors, Dressmakers, Furriers and Milliners
4142	Teachers – Elementary School and Kindergarten
4141	Teachers – Secondary School
6221	Technical Sales Specialists – Wholesale Trade
0131	Telecommunication Carriers Managers
7246	Telecommunications Installation and Repair Workers
7245	Telecommunications Line and Cable Workers
7317	Textile Machinery Mechanics and Repairers
5243	Theatre, Fashion, Exhibit and Other Creative Designers
3144	Therapy and Assessment (other professional occupations)
3235	Therapy and Assessment (other technical occupations)
7283	Tilesetters
7232	Tool and Die Makers
7383	Trades and Related Occupations (other)
5125	Translators, Terminologists and Interpreters
0713	Transportation Managers
Code	**U**
8231	Underground Production and Development Miners
7341	Upholsterers
2153	Urban and Land Use Planners
2282	User Support Technicians
0912	Utilities Managers
Code	**V**
3114	Veterinarians
3213	Veterinary and Animal Health Technologists
Code	**W**
7373	Water Well Drillers
2175	Web Designers and Developers
7265	Welders and Related Machine Operators

Glossary

Anglophone. A native English speaker. Geographical areas can also be referred to as Anglophone or Francophone.

CCIP. Canada Career Information Partnership, a national network of government and private sector agencies which provide career and labour market information to Canadians. See Useful Addresses for contact details.

Chronological CV/résumé. Shows job experience and educational qualifications in date order (from the most recent to the oldest).

College. Post-secondary education, not as advanced as university.

Email. Part of the Internet which allows messages to be sent to and received by individuals with addresses on the system.

Employment Authorisation. A work permit. Issued by the Canadian High Commission.

Federal government. The government of Canada, responsible for country-wide taxation, defence, budgets, law and order.

Francophone. A native French speaker. Geographical areas can also be referred to as Francophone or Anglophone.

Functional CV/résumé. Classifies job experience and educational qualifications by skills.

Gas. Petrol, when used with reference to automobiles.

Governor General of Canada. Represents the Queen in Canadian government, signing Acts of Parliament.

High school. Post-secondary education. Completed before college and/or university.

House of Commons. Elected body of Members of Parliament. Fulfils the same function as the House of Commons in Britain.

Human Resources and Skills Development Centre. Located in cities and towns throughout Canada, these offices are where you register for a Social Insurance Number. They also provide help with job hunting.

Immigration attorney. A solicitor who specialises in legal matters pertaining to immigration and offers services to help intending immigrants obtain employment authorisation and/or Landed Immigrant status.

Immigration consultant. Offers services designed to help the intending immigrant obtain employment authorisation and/or Permanent Resident status and, sometimes, to settle in the new country.

Internet. The world-wide system of electronic communication via computer links.

Medicare. A name often given to the various provincial health insurance schemes.

MLS. Multiple Listing Services. A listing of all properties available through real estate agents.

Permanent Resident. Someone who has been granted immigrant status and is entitled to live and work in Canada as a permanent resident.

PNP. Provincial Nominee Programme by which specific provinces encourage immigration by members of certain trades and professions relevant to their provincial needs.

PRC. Permanent Resident Card. An identity card for immigrants introduced in 2002.

Province. One of the ten separate areas of Canada which enjoy a degree of self-government. Similar to English counties.

Provincial government. The more localised elected government responsible for local taxes, health care, transportation.

Real estate. Land and/or property available to buy and sell. A real estate agent or realtor is called an estate agent in the UK.

Résumé A North American term for a CV.

Senate. A Canadian federal government body, corresponds to the British House of Lords.

SIN. An abbreviation of Social Insurance Number, without which you cannot work legally in Canada. Similar to the British National Insurance number.

Sponsor. A Canadian citizen or permanent resident who is willing to support financially an intending immigrant or temporary worker.

Territory. Similar to a province (see above), exercising a degree of self-government. There are three Territories in Canada.

UIC. Unemployment Insurance Commission. The government body which controls unemployment benefits (these are also referred to by the initials UIC).

Vacation. Holiday.

Visa officer. The immigration official who deals with individual applications.

Website. Accessed via the Internet, the location of comprehensive information on a specific topic.

Further Reading

ABOUT CANADA

Apple's America: The Discriminating Traveller's Guide to 40 Great Cities in the United States and Canada, R W Apple (North Point Press 2005).

Associations Canada: An Encyclopedic Directory (Canadian Almanac & Directory 2005).

Canada (Lonely Planet Country Guides), Andrea Schulte-Peevers et al (Lonely Planet Publications 2005).

Canada DK Eyewitness Travel Guides (DK Publishing 2003).

Canada Green Guide (Michelin Green Guides 2003).

Canada Insight Guide (Insight Guides 2004).

Canada: The Rough Guide, Tim Jepson, Phil Lee, Tania Smith (Rough Guides 2004).

Canada Year Book (Statistics Canada, annual).

Canadian Almanac and Directory (Canadian Almanac and Directory, annual).

Collins Independent Travel Series (Collins 2001).

Culture Shock! A Wife's Guide, Robin Pascoe (Graphic Arts Centre Publishing Co 2004).

Culture Shock! Canada: A Guide to Customs and Etiquette, Robert Barlas et al (Kuperard 2004).

Good Schools Guide (Expat Network 2003).

Living and Working in Canada 2nd edition (How To Books 2003).

Lonely Planet Canada, Mark Lightbody et al (Lonely Planet Publications 2002).

The Migrant Experience (video) (*Canada News* 2001).

The School Solution (Canada Information Services 1995).

So, You Want to Be Canadian: All About the Most Fascinating People in the World and the Magical Place That They Call Home, Kerry Colburn and Rob Sorensen (Chronicle Books 2004).

EMPLOYMENT INFORMATION

Accounting Jobs Worldwide, Ian Collier (Vacation Work 1998).

A future for you in Canada (video) (*Canada News*, 2001).

Associations Canada (Micromedia 2005).

The Ayer Directory of Publications (Ayer, Canada 2005).

Benn's Media Directory (Canada 2005).

(The) Canada Contact Directory (The Expat Network 2005).

Canada's Top 100 Employers (Canada 2005).

Canadian Directory of Search Firms (Mediacorp 2005).

(The) Canadian Key Business Directory (Dun and Bradstreet 2005).

(The) Career Directory (Canada 2005)

The CEPEC Recruitment Guide (CEPEC, annual).

Directory of Executive Management and Development Consultants (Executive Grapevine, annual).

Getting a Job Abroad 7th edition, Roger Jones (How To Books 2003).

Getting into Canada: How to Make a Successful Application for Permanent Residence, Benjamin A Kranc and Elena Constantin (How To Books 2004).

Immigrating to Canada and Finding Employment, Tariq Nadeem (Self-Help Publishers 2003).

International Jobs: Where They Are, How to Get Them, Eric Kocher and Nina Segal (Perseus Books 2003).

Jobs and Careers Abroad, Deborah Penrith (Vacations Works Publications 2005).

Live and Work in the USA and Canada, Victoria Pybus (Vacation Work Publications 2005).

Living & Working in Canada 2nd edition Benjamin A Kranc and Karina Roman (How To Books 2003).

Living and Working in Canada: A Survival Handbook, Janet Macdonald et al (Survival Books 2003).

Market Research Handbook (Statistics Canada, annual).

Planning Your Gap Year 7th edition, Mark Hempshell (How To Books 2005).

Success Secrets to Maximize Business in Canada, Ken Coates (Graphic Arts Center Publications Co 2001).

Summer Jobs Abroad, David Woodworth and Victoria Pybus
(Vacation Work Publications 2005).

Teaching English as a Foreign Language, Sue Tyson-Ward (How
To Books 2000).

What Color is Your Parachute? Richard Nelson Bolles (Ten Speed
Press 1999).

Who Owns Whom (Dun & Bradstreet UK, annual).

Who's Hiring (Canada 2005).

Willing's Press Guide (Canada, 2005).

Working Abroad (Expat Network 2005).

*Working Abroad – Daily Telegraph Guide to Working and Living
Overseas,* Godfrey Golzen (Kogan Page, London, annual).

Worldwide Volunteering 4th edition (How To Books 2004).

Useful Addresses and Websites

ACCOMMODATION

BBCanada (on-line B & B listings) at www.BBCanada.com

Budget Hotels (on-line reservations) at www.budgethotels.com

Canada Bay Properties Inc., 255 Duncan Mill Road, Suite 810, Don Mills, ON M3B 3H9. Tel: (416) 449 1055. Fax: (416) 449 9348. Email: dewji@myna.com

Canadian Real Estate Association, 1600–344 Slater Street, Canada Building, Ottawa, ON KIR 7Y3. Tel: (613) 237 7111. http://realtors.mls.ca/crea/index.htm

Canadian Relocation Systems, 1–456 George Road East, Victoria, BC V8T 2W4. Tel: (250) 480 5543. Email: info@relocatecanada.com

Chloe Cartwright (real estate and temporary accommodation). Tel: (403) 650 0888. www.c21gold.ca

John Clark regarding buying or renting a home in Ontario: www.homesforsalecollection.com email: johnclark@exit4u.com

The Dallimores B & B, Postal Outlet, Box 47019, Quinn Stationary, 2225 Ern Mills Parkway, Mississauga, ON L5K 2P0. Tel/Fax: (905) 823 5212.

Anne Daud, Licensed Real Estate Representative. Tel: (613) 841 5043. Email: an.daudx2@sympatico.ca

Dorrington Bed and Breakfast, 13851–19A Ave, White Rock, BC V4A 9MW. Tel: (604) 535 4408. Fax: (604) 535 4409. Internet: www.bbcanada.com/508.html

Glen Grove Suites, 2837 Yonge street, Toronto, ON M4N 2J6. Tel: (416) 489 8441. Fax: (416) 440 3065.

Helen Willy, Calgary, Alberta. Tel: (403) 254 4586. Fax: (403) 201 4427. www.cadvision.com/willyh Email: willyh@cadvision.com

Multiple Listing Service (Real Estate) at www.mls.ca

Renate Penkett, Re/Max North Park Realty Inc, 79 Bryant St, Oakville, ON L6K 2Z5. Tel: (905) 337 1704. Fax: (905) 337 0503. Email: rpenkett@home.com

Royal Bank of Canada regarding house prices:
www.rbcroyalbank.com/buyingahome/afford

Bev Tonkinson, MaxWell Realty, 3205 380 Canyon Meadows Dr SE, Calgary, AB T2J 7C3. Tel: (403) 278 8899 Fax: (403) 271 9797. Email: ukcalgary@home.com

BETTER BUSINESS BUREAUX

Central and Northern Alberta. Capitol Place, #514, 9707–110 Street, Edmonton, AB T5K 2L9. Tel: (780) 482 2341. Fax: (780) 482 1150. www.edmontonbbb.org
Email: info@edmontonbbb.org

General Website: www.bbb.org

Mainland of British Columbia. #404, 788 Beatty Street, Vancouver, BC V6B 2M1. Tel: (604) 682 2711. Fax: (604) 681 1544. www.bbbvan.org Email: bbbmail@bbbvan.org

Midwestern Ontario. 354 Charles Street, Kitchener, ON N2G 4L5. Tel: (519) 579 3080. Fax: (519) 570 0072. www.bbbmwo.org
Email: inquiry@bbbkitchener.org

Montreal Inc. (Bureau d'Ethique Commerciale de Montreal Inc.), #460, 2055 rue Peel, Montreal, PQ H3A 1V4. Tel: (514) 286 1236. Fax: (514) 849 2658.

Nova Scotia. #601, 1888 Brunswick Street, Halifax, NS B3J 3J8. Tel: (902) 422 6581. Fax: (902) 429 6457. www.bbbns.com
Email: bbbns@bbbns.com

Ottawa and Hull Inc. #603, 130 Albert Street, Ottawa, ON K1P 5G4. Tel: (613) 237 4856. Fax: (613) 237 4878.
www.easternontario.bbb.org
Email: info@easternontario.bbb.org

Quebec Inc. (Bureau d'Ethique Commerciale de Quebec Inc.), 485 rue Richelieu, Quebec, PQ G1R 1K2. Tel: (418) 523 2555. Fax: (418) 523 2444. www.bbb-bec.com.
Email: bbbbec@bbb-bec.com

Saskatchewan Inc. #302, 2080 Broad Street, Regina SK S4P 1Y3. Tel: (306) 352 7601. Fax: (306) 565 6236.
www.saskatchewan.bbb.org
Email: bbbsask@accesscomm.ca

South Central Ontario. 100 King Street East, Hamilton, ON L8N 1A8. Tel: (905) 526 1111. Fax: (905) 526 1225.

www.hamilton.bbb.org Email: bbbhamilton@iprimus.ca

Southern Alberta. #350, 7330 Fisher Street, SE Calgary, AB T2H
2H8. Tel: (403) 531 8780. Fax: (403) 640 2514.
www.betterbusiness.ca Email: info@betterbusiness.ca

Vancouver Island. #201, 1005 Langley Street, Victoria, BC V8W
1V7. Tel: (250) 386 6348. Fax: (250) 386 2367.
www.victoria.bbb.org Email: inquiries@bbbvanisland.org

Western Ontario. 616, 200 Queens Avenue, London, ON N6A
1J3. Tel: (519) 673 3222. Fax: (519) 673 5966.
www.bbblondon.on.ca Email: info@bbblondon.on.ca

Windsor and Southern Ontario. 500 Riverside Drive West,
Windsor, ON N9A 5K4. www.bbbwindsor.com
Email: wbbb@wincom.net

Winnipeg and Manitoba. #301, 365 Hargrave Street, Winnipeg,
MB R3B 2K3. Tel: (204) 943 1486. Fax: (204) 943 1489.
www.manitoba.bbb.org Email: bbb1@mb.sympatico.ca

CANADA CAREER INFORMATION PARTNERSHIP OFFICES (CCIPs)

Canada CIP

National Coordinator, Canada Career Information Partnership,
200 Crichton Street, Ottawa, ON K1M 1V4. Tel: (613) 863
1187. Fax: (613) 745 8284. Email: glarose@ccip-picc.org

Provincial and Territorial CIPs

Alberta. Alberta Human Resources and Employment, 12th Floor,
Seventh Street Plaza, South Tower, 10030–107 Street,
Edmonton, AB T5J 3E4. Tel: (780) 422 5312. Fax: (780) 422
5319.
Email: judy.hutchinson@gov.ab.ca

British Columbia. Student Transitions Standards Unit, British
Columbia Ministry of Education, 4th Floor, 620 Superior
Street, Box 9159 Stn. Prov Govt, Victoria, BC V8W 9H3.
Tel: (250) 387 6398. Fax: 250 356 6161.
Email: paul.lukaszek@gems7.gov.bc.ca

Manitoba. Manitoba Education and Training, 1970 Ness Avenue, Suite W320, Winnipeg, Manitoba R3J 0Y9. Tel: (204) 945 7974. Fax: (204) 948 3668. Email: tprins@gov.mb.ca

New Brunswick. NB Department of Education, Career Development Consultant, Community and Individual Development, Department of Family and Community Services, PO Box 6000, 551 King Street, Fredericton, NB E3B 1E7. Tel: (506) 457 6704. Fax: (506) 453 2869. Email: Judy.Cumberland@gnb.ca

Newfoundland. Division of Student Support Services, Newfoundland and Labrador Department of Education, Confederation Building, PO Box 8700, St John's, NF A1B 4J6. Tel: (709) 729 3008. Email: sandrataylor@gov.nl.ca

Northwest Territories. Department of Education, Culture & Employment, Government of Northwest Territories, PO Box 1320, Yellowknife, NT X1A 2L9. Tel: (867) 920 3191. Fax: (867) 873 0200. Email: catherine_boyd@gov.nt.ca

Nova Scotia. Skills and Learning Branch, Nova Scotia Department of Education, PO Box 578, Halifax, NS B3J 2S9. Tel: (902) 424 5435. Fax: (902) 424 0749. Email: arsenale@gov.ns.ca

Nunavut. Qikiqtani Career and Early Childhood Services, Nunavut Department of Education, PO Box 204, Pangnirtung, NU X0A 0R0. Tel: (867) 473 2600. Fax: (867) 473 2647. Email: sdialla@gov.nu.ca

Ontario. Ministry of Education, 900 Bay Street, 8th Floor, Mowat Block, Toronto, ON M7A 1L2. Tel: (416) 325 7886. Fax: (416) 325 2552. Email: chantal.locatelli@edu.gov.on.ca

Prince Edward Island. Department of Education, Student Services Division, PO Box 2000, Charlottetown, PE C1A 7N8. Tel: (902) 368 4674. Fax: (902) 368 4622. Email: lanoonan@gov.pe.ca

Quebec. English Speaking Community Services, Policies and Projects Department, Ministère de l'Éducation, du Loisir et du Sport du Québec, 600 rue Fullum, 9e Étage Montréal, QC H2K 4L1. Tel: (514) 873 6025. Fax: (514) 864 4181. Email: barbara.goode@mels.gouv.qc.ca

Saskatchewan. 2220 College Avenue, 3rd Floor, Regina, SASK
S4P 3V7. Tel: (306) 787 7382.
Email: jim.savage@sasked.gov.sk.ca

Yukon. Department of Education, Government of Yukon, 1000
Lewes Boulevard, Whitehorse, Yukon Y1A 2C6. Tel: (867) 667
3006. Fax: (867) 393 6339. Email: judith.mcintyre@gov.yk.ca

CHAMBERS OF COMMERCE

London Chamber of Commerce, 33 Queen Street, London EC4R
1AP. Tel: (020) 7248 4444. www.londonchamber.co.uk
Email: lc@londonchamber.co.uk

Canada UK Chamber of Commerce, 38 Grosvenor Street,
London W1K 4DP. Tel: 020 7258 6576. Fax: 020 7258 6594.
www.canada-uk.org Email: info@canada-uk.org

Canadian Chamber of Commerce, Delta Office Tower, 350 Sparks
Street, Suite 501, Ottawa, ON K1R 7S8. Tel: (613) 238 4000.
Fax: (613) 238 7643 www.chamber.ca
Email: info@chamber.ca

CREDENTIAL ASSESSMENT AND ADVICE

Academic Credentials Evaluation Service, 4700 Keele Street,
Toronto, ON M3J 1P3. Tel: (416) 736 2100. www.yorku.ca

Canadian Information Centre for International Credentials, 95
Clair West, Suite 1106, Toronto, Ontario M4V 1N6.
Tel: (416) 962 9725. Fax: (416) 962 2800. www.cicic.ca

Document Evaluation Service, York University, 4700 Keele St,
North York, ON M3J 1P3. Tel: (416) 736 5000.
Fax: (416) 736 5536. Email: dstandic@yorku.can

International Credential Assessment Service of Canada, Inc, ICAS
of Canada, 147 Wyndham Street North, Suite 409, Guelph,
ON N1H 4E9. Tel: (519) 763 7282. www.icascanada.ca
Email: info@icascanada.ca

International Credential Evaluation Service (ICES), 3700
Willingdon Avenue, Burnaby, British Columbia V5G 3H2.
Tel: (604) 432 8800. Fax: (604) 435 7033. www.bcit.ca/ices
Email: icesinfo@bcit.ca

International Qualifications Assessment Service, 9th Floor, 108
  Street Building, 9942–108 Street, Edmonton, Alberta AB T5K
  2J5. Tel: (780) 427 2655. Fax: (780) 422 9734.
  www.advancededucation.gov.ab.ca/iqas/iqas.asp
(Ontario) Comparative Education Service, University of Toronto,
  Admissions & Awards, 315 Bloor St. West, Toronto, Ontario
  M5S 1A3. Tel: (416) 978 2185. www.adm.utoronto.ca

For the Province of Quebec only:
Ministère des Relations avec les Citoyens et de l'Immigration, 360
  rue McGill, Montreal, Quebec H2Y 2E9. Tel: (514) 873 6975.
  Fax: (514) 873 8701. www.immq.gouv.qc.ca

EDUCATION
Canadian Association of Independent Schools, 12 Bannockburn
  Ave, Toronto, ON M5M 2M8. Tel: (416) 780 1779.
  www.cais.ca
Canadian Bureau for International Education, 220 Laurier
  Avenue West, Suite 1550, Ottawa, ON K1P 5Z9. Tel: (613) 237
  4820 Fax: (613) 237 1073. www.cbie.ca
Canadian School Boards Association, 340 Laurier Avenue West,
  PO Box 2095, Ottawa, ON K1P 5W3. Tel: (613) 235 3724.
  Fax: (613) 238 8434. www.cdnsba.org
  Email: admin@cdnsba.org.
Canadian Society for Study of Higher Education at
  www.education.mcgill.ca/csshe
League for the Exchange of Commonwealth Teachers, 7 Lion
  Yard, Tremadoc Road, Clapham, London SW4 7NQ. Tel:
  0870 770 2636. Fax: 0870 770 2637. Email: info@lect.org.uk
Society for Educational Visits & Exchanges in Canada, 57 Auriga
  Dr, Nepean, ON K2E 8B2. Tel: 2 (613) 998 3760. Fax: (613)
  998 7094. www.sevec.ca

EDUCATION OFFICES – PROVINCIAL
Alberta Department of Education. Tel: (780) 427 7219. Email:
  comm.contact@learning.gov.ab.ca and Alberta Advanced
  Education, Tel: (780) 422 5400. Fax: (780) 422 1263.

Email: comm.contact@learning.gov.ab.ca or
222.education.gov.ab.ca

British Columbia Ministry of Education, 620 Superior St, Victoria,
BC V8V 2M4. Fax: (604) 387 3200. www.gov.bc.ca

Manitoba Department of Education and Training, Legislative
Building, 450 Broadway, Winnipeg, MB R3C 0V8.
Tel: (204) 945 3744. Fax: (204) 945 4261.
Email: mgi@gov.mb.ca. www.govmb.ca

New Brunswick Department of Education, PO Box 6000,
Fredericton, NB E3B 5H1. Tel: (506) 453 3678. Fax: (506) 453
3325. www.gnb.ca

Newfoundland Department of Education, Confederation Building,
West Block, Box 8700, St John's, NF A1B 4J6. Tel: (709) 729
5097. Fax: (709) 729 5896. www.ed.gov.nl.ca

Northwest Territories Department of Education, PO Box 1320,
Yellowknife, NT X1A 2L9. Fax: (403) 873 0465.
www.gov.nt.ca

Nova Scotia Department of Education, Box 578, Halifax, NS B3J
2S9. Tel: (902) 424 5168. Fax: (902) 424 0511.
http://ednet.ns.ca

Ontario Ministry of Education and Training, Mowat Block, 900
Bay St, Toronto ON M7A 1L2. Fax: (416) 325 6348.
www.edu.gov.on.ca

Prince Edward Island Department of Education, Box 2000,
Charlottetown, PE C1A 7N8. Fax: (902) 368 4663.
www.gov.pe.ca/educ

Quebec Ministère de l'Education, 1035, rue de la Chevrotiere,
Quebec G1R 5A5. Fax: (418) 646 6561. www.meq.qc.ca

Saskatchewan Department of Education, Training and
Employment, 2220 College Ave, Regina, SASK S4P 3V7.
Fax: (306) 787 2280. http://gtds.gov.sk.ca

Yukon Department of Education, PO Box 2703, Whitehorse, YT
Y1A 2C6. Tel: (867) 667 5141. Fax: (867) 393 6254.
www.education.gov.yt.ca

EMPLOYMENT AND JOB SEARCH

Recruiting internationally

Actual Jobs at www.actualjobs.com

Beechwood Recruitment Ltd, 219 High Street, London W3 9BY.
Tel: (020) 8992 8647. www.softwarejobs.co.uk

Canada Employment Weekly at www.mediacorp2.com

Canada Jobs at www.canada.plusjobs.com

Canadian Career Information Partnership at www.ccic.picc.org

Canadian government job search site at www.jobbank.gc.ca

Dare Human Resources Corporation, 275 Slater Street, Suite 900,
Ottawa, Ontario K1P 5H9. Tel: (613) 233 3152. Fax: (613) 236
3754. www.darectr.com

Drake Executive, Drake International, London.
www.drakeintl.com.

Escape Artist (Job Listings) at www.escapeartist.com/jobs/overseas

Ferman Law, Paulette Courtneidge, 27 Bruton St, London W1J
6QN. Tel: (020) 7499 5702. Fax: (020) 236 2533.
Email: paulette@fermanlaw.com

Find a Job at www.find-a-job-canada.com

Fishnet New Media (Job Listings) at www.ahoy.com

Industry Canada at www.strategis.ic.gc.ca

International Student www.internationalstudent.com/jobsearch/
canada

Job Postings at www.postings.gov.bc.ca

Job Search in Canada at www.job-search-in-canada.com

Jobs Abroad at www.jobsabroad.com

Jobs Canada at www.canada-jobs.com

Nanny Plus at www.nannyplus.com

Overseas Jobs Express at www.overseasjobsexpress.com

Overseas Summer Jobs at www.summerjobs.com

Plus Jobs at www.plusjobs.ca

Shadi Norman, BC. Tel: (604) 320 0962. Fax: (604) 436 0962.
Email: ansnorman@shaw.ca

RWH International Inc, 225–620 Wilson Ave, Toronto ON M3K
1Z3. Tel: (416) 636 3933. Fax: (416) 636 8113.
www.canadusemployment.com
Email: info@canadusemployment.com

RWH International (Placement) at
www.canadausemployment.com
The Job Bus Canada www.jobbus.com

IMMIGRATION ATTORNEYS

Abrans & Krochak, 250 Merton St, Suite 402, Toronto, ON M4S
1B1. Tel: (416) 482 3387. Fax: (416) 482 0647.
Email: emigrate@akcanada.com

Brownstein, Brownstein & Associates, 6000 Cote Des Neiges Suite
590, Montreal, Quebec H3S 1Z8. Tel: (514) 939 9559.
Fax: (514) 939 2289. Email: immigrate@brownsteinlaw.com
www.brownsteinlaw.com

Gary M Ferman, 27 Bruton St, London W1J 6QN. Tel: (020)
7499 5702. Fax: (020) 7236 2533.
Email: fermanlaw@compuserve.com

Goldman Associates, 2nd Floor, St John St, London EC1V 4PY.
Tel: (0800) 028 7508. Email: info@immigrationtocanada.org

Green & Spiegel, Barristers and Solicitors, 390 Bay Street, Suite
2800, Toronto, ON M5H 2Y2. Tel: (416) 862 7880.
Fax: (416) 862 1698. www.gands.com

Karas & Associates, 65 Queen Street West, Suite 1105, Toronto,
ON M5H 2M5. Tel: (416) 506 1800. Fax: (416) 506 1305.
Email: karas@karas.ca

Kranc & Associates, 425, University Avenue, Suite 500, Toronto,
M5G 1T6. Tel: (416) 977 7500. Fax: (416) 977 5200. Email:
bkranc@migratecanada.com

Sheldon M Robins, 60 St Clair Ave East, Suite 1000, Toronto,
ON M4T 1N5. Tel: (416) 963 8888. Fax: (905) 709 1177.
Email: immigrationtocanada@sympatico.ca

Thomas Immigration Law Group, 1885 Marine Drive, North
Vancouver, Vancouver, BC V7P 1V5. Tel: (604) 988 0795.
Fax: (604) 988 0718. www.executive.visa.com
Email: info@executive-visa.com

IMMIGRATION CONSULTANTS

Acadia (Canadian Head Office), 123 Ferrier Avenue 1, Toronto,
ON M4K 3H6. Tel: (416) 778 4975. Fax: (416) 778 7331.
Email: acadia@trigger.net

Acadia, 698 Danforth Avenue, Suite 102, Toronto, ON M4J 1L1.
    Tel: (416) 778 7141. Fax: (416) 778 7331.
    Email: visa@immigrate2000.com
Access Migration Services. Tel: 0845 644 5607. Fax: 01933 384643.
    Email: accessmigration@btconnect.com
Canada Wise, 612–500 Country Hills Blvd NE., Suite 141,
    Calgary, AB T3K 5K3. Tel: (403) 226 4999.
    Fax: (403) 226 1220. Email: info@canadawise.com
Courtneidge Associates, Tel: 07951 399284.
    www.courtneidgeassociates.ca
Emigration Plus (International) Ltd, Hanover House, Hanover
    Street, Liverpool L1 3DZ. Tel: (0151) 285 3830. Fax: (0151)
    285 3863. email: williamcsstanley@emigrationplus.co.uk
Four Corners Emigration, Strathblane House, Ashfield Road,
    Cheadle, Cheshire SK8 1BB. Tel: 0845 8419 453. Fax: (0161)
    608 1616. Email: info@fourcorners.net www.fourcornersnet
Hand in Hand Immigration Ltd, 27 Cavendish Rd, Felixstowe,
    Suffolk IP11 2AR. Tel: (01394) 276379. Fax: (01394) 284102.
    Email: hand_in_hand@hotmail.com
Job Search in Canada, Tel: (604) 320 0962. Fax: (604) 436 0962.
    www.jobsearch-in-canada-com. Email: ansnorman@shaw.ca
SIS Canada Ltd, UK Office, No 1 Olympic Way, Ste 424,
    Wembley Park, Middx HA9 0NP. Tel: (020) 8782 1142/782
    1143. Email: siscanada@yahoo.com

INSURANCE SPECIALISTS
Canadasure, Expatriate Insurance Services, 2 St Mary's Court,
    Carleton Forehoe, Norwich NR9 4AL. Tel: 0870 330 0016.
    Fax: (01603) 757 863. Email: info@expatriate-insurance.com

NEWSPAPERS CANADA NATIONAL
The National Post, 300–1450 Don Mills Rd, Toronto, ON M3B
    2RS. www.nationalpost.com
The Globe and Mail, 444 Front Street West, Toronto, ON M5V
    2S9. www.globeandmail.com

NEWSPAPERS (DAILY) PUBLISHED IN CANADA'S MAJOR CITIES

All these can be accessed on the internet:

Alberta
Calgary. www.canada.com/calgary
The Calgary Sun, www.calgarysun.com
Edmonton. *The Edmonton Journal*, www.canada.com/edmonton/
    edmontonjournal
The Edmonton Sun, www.edmontonsun.com

British Columbia
Vancouver. www.canada.com/vancouver/vancouversun
The Province, Pacific Press Ltd, www.canada.com/vancouver/
    theprovince
Victoria. *Times Colonist*, www.canada.com/victoria/timescolonist

Manitoba
Winnipeg. *Winnipeg Free Press*, www.winnipegfreepress.com
The Winnipeg Sun, www.winnipeg.com/winsun.shtml

New Brunswick
Fredericton. *Daily Gleaner*, www.canadaeast.com
Saint John. *The Telegraph-Journal*, www.canadaeast.com
Times and Transcript, www.canadaeast.com

Newfoundland
St John's. *The Evening Telegram*, www.thetelegram.com

Nova Scotia
Halifax. *The Chronicle-Herald*, www.herald.ns.ca
The Daily News, www.hfxnews.com
Sydney. *Cape Breton Post*, www.capebretonpost.com

Ontario
Kingston. www.thewhig.com
Ottawa. *Le Droit*, www.cyberpresse.ca/droit

The Ottawa Citizen, www.canada.com/ottawa/ottawacitizen
Ottawa Sun, ottawa.com/ottsun.shtml
The Toronto Star, www.thestar.com
The Toronto Sun, www.torontosun.com

Prince Edward Island
Charlottetown. *Charlottetown Guardian*, www.theguardian.pe.ca

Quebec
Montreal. *Le Devoir*, www.ledevoir.com
The Gazette, www.canada.com/montreal/montrealgazette
Le Journal de Montreal, www.journaldequebec.com
La Presse, www.cyberpresse.ca
Quebec. *Le Journal de Quebec*, www.journaldequebec.com
Le Soleil, www.cyberpresse.com

Saskatchewan
Regina. *The Leader-Post*, www.canada.com/regina/leaderpost
Saskatoon. *Star-Phoenix*, www.canaca.com/saksatoon/starphoenix

Yukon & Northwest Territories
Whitehorse. *The Daily Star*, www.whitehorsestar.com
Yellowknife. *L'Aquilon* www.aquilon.nt.ca
News/North, www.nnsl.com
Yellowknifer, www.nnsl.com

OCCUPATIONAL TRAINING – FEDERAL DEPARTMENTS
Centre For Professional Development, PO Box 420, Ottawa, ON
    K1N 8V4. Tel: (613) 997 4163. Fax: (613) 953 6240.
Human Resources Development Canada, Communications, Place
    du Portage, Phase IV, 140 Promenade du Portage, Hull, PQ
    K1A 0J9. Tel: (819) 994 6013. www.hdrc-drhc.gc.ca
Public Service Commission of Canada, Training Programs
    Branch, Ottawa, ON K1A 0M7. Tel: (613) 992 9562.
    Fax: (613) 954 7561. www.psc-cfp.gc.ca

PET TRAVEL SPECIALISTS

Airpets Oceanic, Willowslea Kennels, Spout Lane North, Stanwell
Moor, Staines, Middlesex TW19 6BW. Tel: (01753) 685 571.
Fax: (01753) 681 655. Email: info@airpets.com
www.airpets.com

Animal Airlines, Mill Lane Cottage, Mill Lane, Adlington,
Cheshire. Tel: (01625) 827414. Fax: (01625) 827237.
www.animalairlines.co.uk
Email: enquiries@animalairlines.co.uk

Golden Arrow Shippers, Lydbury North, Shropshire, SY7 8DY.
Tel: (01588) 680 240. Fax: (01588) 680 414.

Par Air Livestock Shipping Services, Stanway, Colchester, Essex
CO3 0LN. Tel: (01206) 330332. Fax: (01206) 331277.
www.parair.co.uk Email: parair@btinternet.com

Transpet, 160 Chingford Mount Road, Chingford, London E4
9BS. Tel: (020) 8529 0979. Fax: (020) 8529 2563.
www.transpetonline.com

PROFESSIONAL ASSOCIATIONS – CANADA

Accounting

Canadian Association of Certified Executive Accountants, 3030
Southmore Ave E, Ottawa, ON K1B 6Z4. www.cacea.ca

Canadian Institute of Chartered Accountants, 277 Wellington
Street West, Toronto, ON M5V 3H2. Tel: (416) 977 3222.
Fax: (416) 977 8585. www.cica.ca

Advertising and marketing

Canadian Institute of Marketing, 205 Miller Drive, Georgetown,
ON. Tel: (905) 877 5369. Fax: (905) 702 0819.
www.cinstmarketing.ca

Agriculture and farming

Agricultural Institute of Canada, 280 Albert Street, Suite 900,
Ottawa, ON K1P 5G8. Tel: (613) 232 9459 ext 300. Fax: (613)
594 5190. www.aic.ca. Email: office@aic.ca

Canadian Federation of Agriculture, #1101, 75 Albert Street, Ottawa, ON K1P 5E7. Tel: (613) 236 3633. Fax: (613) 236 5749. www.cfa-fca.ca

Animal breeding
Canadian Cattlemen's Association, #310, 6715–8th St. NE, Calgary, AB T2E 7H7. Tel: (403) 275 8558. Fax: (403) 274 5686. www.cattle.ca

Animals and animal science
Canadian Veterinary Medical Association, 339 Booth Street, Ottawa, ON K1R 7K1. Tel: (613) 236 1162. Fax: (613) 236 9681. www.canadianveterinarians.net
Email: info@canadianveterinarians.net

Architecture
Royal Architectural Institute of Canada, #330, 55 Murray Street, Ottawa, ON K1N 5M3. Tel: (613) 241 3600. Fax: (613) 241 5750. www.raic.org

Automotive
Automotive Industries Association of Canada, 1272 Wellington Street, Ottawa, ON K1Y 3A7. Tel: (613) 728 5821. Fax: (613) 728 6021. www.aiacanada.com Email: aia@aiacanada.com

Aviation and aerospace
Aerospace Industries Association of Canada, #1200, 60 Queen Street, Ottawa, ON K1P 6Y7. Tel: (613) 232 4297. Fax: (613) 232 1142. www.aiac.ca Email: info@aiac.ca

Broadcasting
Canadian Association of Broadcasters, PO Box 627, Station B, Ottawa, ON K1P 5S2. Tel: (613) 233 4035. Fax: (613) 233 6961. www.cab-acr.ca Email: cab@cab-acr.ca

Building and construction

Canadian Construction Association, #400, 75 Albert Street, Ottawa, ON K1P 5E7. Tel: (613) 236 9455. Fax: (613) 236 9526. www.cca-acc.com

Chemical industry

Canadian Chemical Producers' Association, #805, 350 Sparks Street, Ottawa, ON K1R 7S8. Tel: (613) 237 6215. Fax: (613) 237 4061. www.ccpa.ca Email: info@ccpa.ca

Consumers

Canadian Society of Consumer Affairs Professionals in Business, #356, 5694 Highway 7 East Markham, ON L3P 1B4. www.socapcanada.org Email: info@socapcanada.org

Dental

Canadian Dental Association, 1815 Alta Vista Drive, Ottawa, ON K1G 3Y6. Tel: (613) 523 1770. Fax: (613) 523 7736. www.cda-adc.ca

Economics

Department of Economics, University of Toronto, 150 St. George Street, Toronto, ON M5S 3G7. Tel: (416) 978 4603. Fax: (416) 978 6713. www.economics.utoronto.ca

Education

Association of Universities & Colleges of Canada, #600, 350 Albert Street, Ottawa, ON K1R 1B1. Tel: (613) 563 1236. Fax: (613) 563 9745. www.aucc.ca

Canadian Education Association, #300, 317 Adelaide Street West, Toronto, ON M5V 1P9. Tel: (416) 591 6300. Fax: (416) 591 5345. www.acea.ca

Energy

Canadian Institute of Energy, #229, 3064 St. Kilda Avenue North, Vancouver, BC V7N 2A9. Tel: (604) 904 5777. www.cienergy.org Email: info@cienergy.org

Engineering and technology

Canadian Council of Professional Engineers, #1100, 180 Elgin Street, Ottawa, ON K2P 2K3. Tel: (613) 232 2474. www.ccpe.ca

Film and video

Canadian Film & Television Production Association, 160 John Street, 5th Floor, Toronto, ON M5V 2E5. Tel: (416) 304 0280. Fax: (416) 304 0499. Also 1140 Homer Street, Suite 301, Vancouver, BC V6B 2X6. Tel: (604) 682 8619. Fax: (604) 684 9294.

Fisheries and fishing industry

Fisheries Council of Canada, 900–170 Laurier Avenue West, Ottawa, ON K1P 5V5. Tel: (613) 727 7450. Fax: (613) 727 7458. www.fisheriescouncil.ca

Food and beverage industry

See Agriculture and Agri-Food Canada http://atn-riae.agr.ca

Forestry and forest products

Canadian Forestry Association, Tel: (613) 732 2917. Fax: (613) 732 3386. www.canadianforestry.com

Gas and oil

Petroleum Services Association of Canada, 1150, 800 6th Avenue South West, Calgary, AB T2P. Tel: (403) 264 4195. Fax: (403) 263 7174. www.psac.ca

Health and medical

The Canadian Medical Association, 1867 Alta Vista Drive, Ottawa, ON K1G 5W8. Tel: (613) 731 9331. Fax: (613) 236 8864. www.cma.ca

Hospitals

Canadian Healthcare Association, 17 York Street, Ottawa, ON
  K1N 9J6. Tel: (613) 241 8005. Fax: (613) 241 5053.
  www.canadian-healthcare.org

Information technology

Information Technology Association of Canada, #404, 2800
  Skylark Avenue, Mississauga, ON L4W 5A6. Tel: (905) 602
  8345. Fax: (905) 602 8346. www.itac.ca. email: info@itac.ca

Insurance industry

Insurance Brokers Association of Canada, 1230–155 University
  Avenue, Toronto, ON M5H 3B7. Tel: (416) 367 1831.
  Fax: (416) 367 3687. www.ibac.ca email: info@ibac.ca

Law

Canadian Bar Association, 500–865 Carling Avenue, Ottawa, ON
  K1S 5S8. Tel: (613) 237 2925 or (613) 237 1988. Fax: (613) 237
  0185. www.cba.org

Management and administration

Institute of Chartered Secretaries & Administrators in Canada,
  #255, 55 St Clair Avenue West, Toronto, ON M4V 2Y7.
  Tel: (416) 944 9727. Fax: (416) 967 6320. www.icsacanada.org

Manufacturing

Canadian Manufacturers and Exporters, 75 International
  Boulevard, 4th Floor, Toronto, ON M4W 6L9. Tel: (416) 798
  8000. Fax: (416) 798 8050. www.cme-mec.ca

Mines and mineral products

Canadian Institute of Mining, Suite 855, 3400 de Maisonneuve
  Boulevard W, Montreal, QC H3Z 3B8. Tel: (514) 939 2710.
  Fax: (514) 939 2714. www.cim.org

Nursing
Canadian Nurses Association, 50 The Driveway, Ottawa, ON K2P 1E2. Tel: (613) 237 2133. Fax: (613) 237 2714. www.cin-nurses.cra

Pharmaceutical
Canadian Pharmaceutical Association, 1785 Alta Vista Drive, 2nd Floor, Ottawa, ON K1P 3Y6. Tel: (613) 523 7877. Fax: (613) 523 0445. www.cdnpharm.ca

Printing industry and graphic arts
Canadian Printing Industries Association, #906, 75 Albert Street, Ottawa, ON K1P 5E7. Tel: (613) 236 7208. Fax: (613) 236 8169. www.cpia-aci.ca

Publishing
Association of Canadian Publishers, 110 Eglinton Avenue West, #401, Toronto, ON M4R 1A3. Tel: (416) 487 6116. Fax: (416) 487 8815. www.publishers.ca

Real estate
The Canadian Real Estate Association, #1600, Minto Place, The Canada Building, 344 Slater Street, Ottawa, ON K1R 7Y3. Tel: (613) 237 7111. Fax: (613) 234 2567. www.crea.ca

Restaurants, bars, food services
Canadian Restaurant & Foodservices Association, #1202, 316 Bloor Street West, Toronto, ON M5W 1W5. Tel: (416) 923 8416. Fax: (416) 923 1450. www.crfa.ca Email: info@crfa.ca

Retail trade
Retail Merchants Association of Canada Inc, 1595 16th Avenue, Suite 103, Richmond Hill, ON L4B 3N9. Tel: (905) 764 0893. Fax: (905) 764 8312. www.rmacanada.com Email: info@rmabuydirect.com

Steel and metal industries

Canadian Steel Trade & Employment Congress, #501, 234 Eglinton Avenue East, Toronto, ON M4P 1K7. Tel: (416) 480 1797. Fax: (416) 480 2986. www.cstec.ca Email: general@cstec.ca

Tourism and travel

Tourist Industry Association of Canada, 803–130 Albert Street, Ottawa, ON K1P 5G4. Tel: (613) 238 3883. Fax: (613) 238 3878. www.tiac.aitc.ca

Transportation

Canadian Institute of Traffic & Transportation, 10 King Street East, 4th Floor, Toronto, ON M5E 1G4. Tel: (416) 363 5696. Fax: (416) 363 5698. www.citt.ca

PROVINCIAL NOMINEE PROGRAMME CONTACTS

Alberta. Provincial Nominee Program, Economic Immigration, Alberta Economic Development, 6th Floor, Commerce Place, 10155-102 St, Edmonton, AB T5J 4L6. www.alberta-canada.com.pnp

British Columbia. Provincial Nomination Program, Ministry of Community, Aborginal & Women's Service, PO Box 9915 Stn Prov Gov, Victoria, BC V8W 9V1. www.mcaws.gov.bc.ca/amip/pnp/

Manitoba. Provincial Nominee Program, Immigration Promotion & Recruitment Branch, Labour & Immigration Manitoba, 9th Flr, 213 Notre Dame Ave, Winnpeg, MN R3B 1N3. www.gov.mb.ca/labour/immigrate/english/immigration/1.html

New Brunswick. Provincial Nominee Program, Investment & Immigration, PO Box 6000, Fredericton, NB E3B 5H1. www.gnb/ca/immigration/english/index.htm

Newfoundland and Labrador. Provincial Nominee Program, PO Box 8700, St John's, NF A1B 4J6. www.nlpnp.ca

Nova Scotia. Provincial Nominee Program, The Office of Economic Development, PO Box 2311, 14th Floor South, Maritime Centre, 1505 Barrington Street, Halifax, NS B3J 3C8. www.gov.ns.ca/econ.nsnp

Prince Edward Island. Provincial Nominee Program, Immigration
  & Investment Division, PEI Department of Development and
  Technology and Island Investment Development Inc., PO Box
  1176, 94 Euston St, 2nd Floor, Charlottetown, PEI, C1A 7M8.
  www.gov.pe.ca/immigration
Saskatchewan. Provincial Nominee Program, Department of
  Government Relations and Immigration, Immigration branch,
  2nd Flr, 1919 Saskatchewan Drive, Regina, SK S4P 3V7.
  www.immigrationsask.gov.sk.ca
Yukon. Provincial Nominee Program, Business Immigration,
  Industry Development Business, Tourism and Culture, PO Box
  2703, Whitehorse, YK Y1A 2C6.
  www.economicdevelopment.gov.yk.ca

RELOCATION SPECIALISTS

Canada Wise, Suite 141, 612-500 Country Hills Blvd NE, Calgary,
  AB T3K 5K3. Tel: (403) 226 4999. Fax: (403) 226 1220.
  www.canadawise.com Email: info@canadawise.com
Canilink Relocation, 48 Chapparal Drive SE, Calgary, AB.
  Tel: (403) 254 8051. Email: Canilink@shaw.ca
Emigration Plus (International) Ltd, Tel: (0151) 285 3830.
  Fax: (0151) 285 3863.
  Email: williamcstanley@emigrationplus.co.uk
Four Corners Emigration, Strathblane House, Ashfield Rd,
  Cheadle, Cheshire SK8 1BB. Tel: (0845) 841 9453. Fax: (0161)
  608 1616. Email: info@fourcorners.net
Relocation2BC, Sue and Frank Gerryts. Tel: (604) 763 3563.
  www.relocation2bc.com Email: sue@relocation2BC.com
Renate Penkett, Re/Max North Park Realty Inc, 79 Brant St,
  Oakville, ON L6K 2ZS. Tel: (905) 337 1704. Fax: (905) 337
  0503. Email: rpenkett@cogeco.ca
  www.relocateontario.com/world
Helen Willy, Tel: (403) 995 1858. Fax: (403) 995 1859.
  www.homeiscanada.com Email: helenwil@telus.net

REMOVAL INTERNATIONAL

Abels, branches throughout the UK. Tel: (freephone) (0800) 626
  769. www.abels.co.uk Email: enquiries@abels.co.uk

Allied Pickfords, Heritage House, 345 Southbury Rd, Enfield EN1
  1UP. Tel: Freephone (0800) 289 229. (020) 8219 8000. Fax:
  (020) 8219 8001. www.alliedpickfords.com

Anglo Pacific Int plc. Tel: (020) 8838 8095.
  www.anglopacific.co.uk

Avalon Overseas, Drury Way, Brent Park, London SW8 4UG.
  Freephone: (08080) 282 566.
  Email: avalon@teamrelocation.com

Bishop's Move, branches throughout the UK. Overseas division:
  Freephone: (0800) 616 425.
  Email: overseas@bishopsmove.co.uk

Britannia Movers International. Tel: (0845) 600666.
  Email: international@britannia-movers.co.uk.

Burke Bros, Burke Bros Trading Estate, Foxs Lane,
  Wolverhampton WV1 1PA. Tel: 0800 413256.
  www.burkebros.co.uk Email: sales@burkebros.co.uk.

Crown Relocations, Security House, Abbey Wharf Industrial
  Estate, Kingsbridge Road, Barking, Essex IG11 0BD. Tel:
  (020) 8591 3388. Fax: (020) 8594 4571. www.crownrelo.com

Doree Bonner International, 19 Kennet Road, Dartford, Kent
  DA1 4QN. Freephone: 0800 289 541. Tel: (020) 8303 6261.
  www.doreebonner.co.uk Email: moving@dbonner.co.uk

Excess International Removals, 4 Hannah Close, Great Central
  Way, London NW10 0UX. Tel: (020) 8324 2057. Fax: (020)
  8324 2048. www.excess-international.com
  Email: removals@excess-international.com

Fox International, Block C, Mill Race Lane, Stourbridge, DY8
  1YL. Tel: 0800 132370. Fax: (01384) 440520.
  www.foxmovingcom Email: international@fox-moving.com

John Mason International, 6 Mill Lane Trading Estate, Mill
  Lane, Croydon, Surrey CR1 4AA. Tel: (020) 8667 1133.
  Fax: (020) 8666 0567. www.johnmason.com
  Email: sales@johnmason.com.

PSS International Removals, 1–3 Pegasus Rd, Croydon, Surrey
   CR9 4PS. Tel: (0800) 614508. Email: sales@p-s-s.co.uk
   www.pss.uk.com
Robinsons, Nuffield Way, Abingdon, Oxon OX14 1TN. Tel:
   (0800) 833638. Email: international@robinsons-intl.com
Seven Seas, Tel: 0800 216698. www.sevenseasworldwide.com

TEMPORARY/HOLIDAY WORK: INFORMATION AND ASSISTANCE

BUNAC (British Universities North American Club), 16 Bowling
   Green Lane, London, EC1R 0QH. Tel: (020) 7251 3472. Fax:
   (020) 7251 0215. www.bunac.org Email: enquiries@bunac.org

TOURIST BOARDS – PROVINCIAL

Alberta Tourism, City Centre, 3rd Floor 10155 102nd Street,
   Edmonton, Alberta T5J 4L6. Tel: (403) 427 4321. Fax: (403)
   427 0867. www.traveltoalberta.com
Tourism British Columbia, 812 Wharf Street, Victoria, British
   Columbia V8W 2X2. Tel: (800) 663 6000. Fax: (604) 688 3334.
   www.travel.bc.ca
Travel Manitoba, Department 20, 155 Carlton Street, 7th Floor,
   Winnipeg, Manitoba R3C 3H8. Tel: (204) 945 3777. Fax: (204)
   948 2517. www.gov.mb.ca/Travel-Manitoba
   www.travelmanitoba.com
Tourism New Brunswick, PO Box 12345, Fredericton, New
   Brunswick E3B 5C3. Tel: (800) 561 0123. Fax: (506) 789 2044.
   www.tourismnewbrunswick.ca
Newfoundland and Labrador Tourism Branch, PO Box 8700, St.
   John's, Newfoundland A1B 4K2. Tel: (709) 729 2830. Fax:
   (709) 729 1965. www.gov.nf.ca Email: info@tourism.gov.nf.ca
TravelArctic, PO Box 1320, Yellowknife, Northwest Territories
   X1A 2L9. Tel: (800) 661 0788. Fax: (403) 873 2801.
   www.nwttravel.nt.ca
Nova Scotia Department of Tourism and Culture, PO Box 130,
   Halifax, Nova Scotia B3M 2M7. Tel: (902) 424 5781.
   Fax: (902) 424 2668. www.novascotia.com
   Email: explore@gov.ns.ca

Ontario Travel, Queens Park, Toronto, ON. Tel: (519) 873 4487.
    Fax: (519) 873 4061. www.ontariotravel.net
Prince Edward Island Department of Tourism and Parks, PO Box
    940, Charlottetown, Prince Edward Island C1A 7M5.
    Tel: (902) 368 4444. Fax: (902) 629 2428. www.peiplay.com
Tourisme Quebec, C.P. 979, Quebec 83C ZW3. Tel: (514) 266
    5687. Fax: (514) 864 3838. www.tourisme.gouv.qc.ca
    and www.bonjourquebec.qc.ca
    Email: info@bonjourquebec.qc.ca
Tourism Saskatchewan, 1919 Saskatchewan Drive, Regina,
    Saskatchewan S4P 3V7. Tel: (306) 787 9600. Fax: (306) 787
    5744. www.sasktourism.sk.ca
    Email: travelinfo@sasktourism.com
Tourism Yukon, PO Box 2703, Whitehorse, Yukon Y1A 2C6.
    Tel: (867) 667 5036. Fax: (867) 393 8566. www.touryukon.com
    Email: vacation@gov.yk.ca

TRADE UNIONS – GENERAL
Canadian Federation of Labour, 107 Sparks Street, Suite 300,
    Ottawa, ON K1P 5B5. Tel: (613) 234 4141. Fax (613) 234
    5188. www.xpdnc.com
Canadian Labour Congress, 2841 Riverside Drive, Ottawa, ON
    K1V 8X7. Tel: (613) 521 3400. Fax: (613) 521 4655.
    www.clc-ctc.ca
Confederation des syndicats nationaux, 1601 ave de Lorimier,
    Montreal, PQ H2K 4M5. Tel: (514) 598 2121. Fax: (514) 598
    2089. www.csn.qc.ca

OTHER USEFUL ADDRESSES AND WEBSITES
Bed and Breakfasts & Businesses in BC (British Canadian
    Investments) Email: businesses@embarkation.biz
Business Development of Canada at www.bdc.ca
Business Information at www.bdc.ca
CA Magazine at www.cma-canada.org
Canada Information Services, Suite 421, 253 College St, Toronto,
    ON M5T 1R5. www.nlc-bnc.ca/cainfo/ecaninfo
Canada News at www.outboundpublishing.com

Canada Online (lots of information about Canada) at
www.canadaonline.about.com
Canadasure (insurance specialists) at www.canadasure.com
Canadian Almanac and Directory at
www.mmltdf.com/Directories.Cdn-Almanac.htm
Canadian Alternative (various information) at
www.canadianalternative.com
Canadian Bureau for International Education at www.cbie.ca
Canadian Heritage Dept at www.canadianheritage.gc.ca
Canadian High Commission, Immigration Section, 38 Grosvenor
Street, London W1K 4AA. Tel: (020) 7258 6600. Fax: (020)
7258 6506. www.canada.org.uk
Canadian Weather Info at www.theweathernetwork.com
Capital Health Authority at www.cha.ab.ca
Careers; education, training facilities, jobs and immigration
around the globe at www.careertips.com
Citizen and Immigrations Services at www.cic.ga.ca
Citizenship and Immigration at www.canada.org.uk
Department for Environment, Food and Rural Affairs (general
enquiries), Library Enquiry Desk, Room 320, Nobel House, 17
Smith Square, London SW1P 3JR. Tel: (08459) 335577.
Email (helpline): helpline@defra.gsi.gov.uk www.gov.uk
Expat Network, International House, 500 Purley Way, Croydon,
Surrey CR9 4NZ. Tel: (020) 8760 5100.
www.expatnetwork.com
Farnham Castle International Briefing and Conference Centre,
Farnham Castle, Surrey GU9 0AG. Tel: (01252) 721 194.
Fax: (01252) 711 283. www.farnhamcastle.com
Email: info@farnhamcastle.com
Government of Alberta at www.gov.ab.ca/
Government of BC at www.gov.bc.ca/
Government of Canada's information site at www.canada.gc.ca/
Government of Manitoba at www.gov.mb.ca/
Government of New Brunswick at www.gov.nb.ca/
Government of Newfoundland/Labrador at www.gov.nf.ca/
Government of the Northwest Territories at www.gov.nt.ca
Government of Nova Scotia at www.gov.ns.ca/
Government of Nunuvat at http://npc.nunavut.com

Government of Ontario at www.gov.on.ca/

Government of Prince Edward Island at www.gov.pe.ca/

Government of Quebec at www.gouv.gc.ca/

Government of Saskatchewan at www.gov.sk.ca/

HSBC (regarding Immigrant Investor Programme) www.hsbc.ca/
capital

Immigration Canadian Immigration (a report by migrants for
migrants) at www.immigrationstory.com

Life Abroad at www.lifeabroad.co.uk

Migrate Canada at www.migratecanada.com

Moving Publications Ltd, 44 Upjohn St, Ste 100, Don Mills, ON
M3B 2W1. Tel: (416) 441 1168. Fax: (416) 441 1641.

Moving To Consumer Guides at www.movingto.com

NuCanada (relocation info) at www.nucanada.com

Royal Bank of Canada (regarding Immigrant Investor
Programme) www.rbcprivatebanking.com/canadian-immigrant-
investor-program.html
Email: gpbimmigrantinvestor@rbc.com.

Service d'Immigration du Quebec, Délégation générale du
Quebec, 87/89 rue de La Boetie, 75008 Paris, France. Tel: (33)
153984545. Fax: (33) 153934540.

Statistics Canada at www.statcan.ca

Tourist Information at www.etourist.ca

Training and Careers (Canadian government website) at
www.jobsetc.ca

Transatlantic Transfers Inc (Tax and Financial Advice), 67 Yonge
St, Suite 502, Toronto, ON M5E 1J8. Tel: (416) 815 0076.
Fax: (416) 361 0728. www.transatlantictransfers.com
Email: contact@TransAtlanticTransfers.com.

Work Permit (Immigration information) at workpermit.com/
canada/canada.htm

Index